# ROCKHOUNDING & PROSPECTING

## UPPER MIDWEST

**Jim Magnuson**

Adventure Publications
Cambridge, Minnesota

# DEDICATION

To our dearest son Nicholas, you are forever in our hearts. In you, God gave us the greatest gift: your warmth, beauty, humor and laughter, endless curiosity, and depth of understanding about so many things, and most of all your care for others. You gave of yourself so that others might live and love and laugh. Thank you, Nick!

Edited by Dan Downing
Cover and book design by Jonathan Norberg

Cover photos by Jim Magnuson unless otherwise noted.
**Front:** Don Bendickson/Shutterstock.com: tool inset; Evgeny Haritonov/Shutterstock.com: hammer and rocks; and Steven Schremp/Shutterstock.com: tree background.

All photos by **Jim Magnuson** unless otherwise noted.
**KLM Photo:** 103 (middle), 120 (top), 122 (bottom right), 124 (bottom), 126 (all), 127 (top left and top right), 129 (bottom 3 images); **Diane Magnuson:** 43 (top), 264; **Doug Moore:** 48, 49, 52 (both); **Jonathan Norberg:** 161; **Steve Olson:** 25, 93 (top); and **Erik Rasmussen:** 58, 63, 64, 67 (all), 68, 69, 70 (both top images), 71 (bottom), 72 (all), 73 (all), 74, 260 (bottom).

Images used under license from Shutterstock.com:
**Ambartsumian Valery:** 179 (right); **AMB-MD Photography:** 20; **Anton Ukolov:** 104 (top); **Beekeepx:** 41; **Craig Sterken:** 21 (left); **ehrlif:** 22 (bottom left); **Jacob Boomsma:** 37; **Kees Zwanenburg:** 22 (bottom right); **Lkoimages:** 185 (bottom); **MaxKrav:** 45 (top); **Melinda Nagy:** 244; **melissamn:** 38 (top left); **Mist8881:** 38 (top right); **mooremedia:** 22 (top right); **Nosov Dmitry:** 38 (bottom left); **Piotr Zimniak:** 21 (right); **Rabbit Life:** 38 (bottom right); **Swardian:** 225; **Tami Freed:** 111 (bottom); and **Wildnerdpix:** 22 (top left).

The regulations and approximate equipment pricing referenced in this book are accurate at the time of printing, but they can change, so consult with the appropriate websites/authorities before heading out into the field.

10 9 8 7 6 5 4 3 2 1
**Rockhounding & Prospecting: Upper Midwest: How to Find Gold, Copper, Agates, Thomsonite & Other Favorites**
Copyright © 2021 by Jim Magnuson
Published by Adventure Publications, an imprint of AdventureKEEN
310 Garfield Street South
Cambridge, Minnesota 55008
(800) 678-7006
www.adventurepublications.net
Printed in the United States of America
ISBN 978-1-59193-945-0 (pbk.); ISBN 978-1-59193-946-7 (ebook)

# TABLE OF CONTENTS

# INTRODUCTION

It's easy and fun to dream of plentiful and reliable hunting grounds for highly sought-after gems, minerals, and fossils, but in the 21$^{st}$ century, these dreams quickly meet reality. Novice and even experienced rockhounds often find that once-productive hunting grounds have been privatized, marked as legally pro-tected, reclaimed by some natural force such as overgrowth, or substantially depleted. These factors represent frustrating barriers to successful hunting, but they provide the opportunity for further adventure in discovering untapped sources. The entire experience can be enriched by learning about the natural forces that created, processed, shaped, and distributed those things that we seek with such enthusiasm and diligence. You might even discover a completely new source or deposit of your given quarry, or at least some lightly traveled paths. Those willing to see the prospecting experience in this way will reap ample hard-earned rewards—including the valuable knowledge that experienced hunters won't readily divulge.

All of these reasons make intensive prospecting an important part of successful hunting ventures. Prospecting for some of the more rare and valuable gems, minerals, and fossils can take years to become reliably productive and may also require significant investments in equipment, travel, or obtaining of legal rights to hunt, collect, and extract these treasures. We have learned this the hard way on more than one occasion, spending thousands of dol-lars and significant amounts of time and travel, only to come away empty-handed and frustrated. To use a fishing analogy: there are endless acres of water to fish, but precious few are reliably productive. This explains

the purpose of this book—to inform and guide you in making good choices about where to invest your time and dollars, and to help you understand the kinds of hunting and prospecting that you will personally enjoy. And it is why we will focus on the field experience, both through text and through images that show you the hunting environment, the processes, and the specimens and materials as they are found.

Personal safety is an important yet often overlooked aspect of the prospecting and rockhounding hobby. Risk factors include: wildlife, weather, physical stresses such as exhaustion or dehydration, mining and equipment accidents, and sometimes human (and even criminal) activities. All of these are amplified when you are prospecting and hunting in remote areas, especially when alone. We point out the relevant safety concerns within each chapter and provide suggestions on how to manage them.

This book strives to provide the best and most current information about known prospecting and collecting locales for the given gems, minerals, and fossils. We provide realistic assessments about the quality and quantity of materials that can be found or extracted once you have done the hard work of prospecting and are properly equipped. The processing methods and tools will focus on basics that can be readily learned and applied by amateur hobbyists.

This book doesn't provide detailed maps with specific locations of where to hunt. And bear in mind that information provided in this book may change, so you must always verify with local authorities or landowners whether a location is still open for hunting. We also don't provide detailed information about gem, mineral, and fossil formation, nor intensive details about identification and classification of different materials, as there are many great books that focus on these topics. Similarly, the Lapidary Arts chapter is intended to be introductory, as there are comprehensive publications available.

A valuable resource for learning about and keeping up-to-date with what's happening in the ever-changing world of gem and mineral prospecting is the American Federation of Mineralogical Societies. Consider joining this organization, and even if you don't, make sure to read and learn their published Code of Ethics at this link: amfed.org/ethics.htm

## ABOUT THE GEMS AND MINERALS IN THIS BOOK

The tables on the next page provide an overview of the prospecting areas for the gems and minerals in this book and what the overall prospecting experience is like. Remember that some of these materials and specimens will be quite scarce, and it's unlikely that you'll be able to extract and process them at a profit. Most amateur prospectors and rockhounds view their pursuits purely as a hobby, similar to catch-and-release fishing; it's about the thrill of the hunt, honing and perfecting their skills, and sharing their treasures with others.

**Prospecting Areas**

| Specimen Type | Prospecting Location |
|---|---|
| Lake Superior agates | Multiple hunting ranges across MN, WI, MI, IA |
| Fluorescent sodalite | Upper Peninsula of MI |
| Thomsonite | North shore of Lake Superior in MN |
| Copper | Upper Peninsula of MI, northern WI |
| Gold | Western SD, northeastern MN, northern WI |
| Keokuk geodes | Southeastern IA, northeastern MO, and west-central IL |
| Fairburn, Teepee Canyon, Scenic black, bubblegum, and prairie agates | Western SD |
| Petoskey stones | northern MI, especially near the shorelines of Lake Michigan and Lake Huron |
| Greenstone and datolite | Upper Peninsula of MI |

**Prospecting Summary**

| Specimen Type | Physical Difficulty | Ratio of Prospecting to Hunting | Access to Hunting Sites | Safety Risk | Cost |
|---|---|---|---|---|---|
| Lake Superior agates | Medium | 25:75 | Medium | Low | Low |
| Fluorescent sodalite | Low | 25:75 | High | Low | Low |
| Thomsonite | Medium | 10:90 | Medium | Low | Medium |
| Copper | Medium | 25:75 | Medium | Medium | Medium |
| Gold | Medium | 25:75 | High | Low | Medium |
| Keokuk geodes | Low–Medium | 10:90 | High | Low | Low |
| Fairburn, Scenic black, bubblegum, and prairie agates | Medium | 25:75 | High | Low | Low |
| Teepee Canyon agates | High | 10:90 | High | Medium–High | Low |
| Petoskey stones | Low | 10:90 | High | Low | Low |
| Greenstone and datolite | Medium | 40:60 | Medium | Low | Low |

# LAKE SUPERIOR AGATES

Lake Superior agates (or "lakers") are one of the best-known types of agates. Agates are a form of banded chalcedony, a mineral composed of cryptocrystalline quartz. They primarily form as nodules within air pockets in cooled lava flows. In the Lake Superior area, these lava flows occurred around 1 billion years ago, during an event called the Midcontinent Rift, and they hardened into the basalt and rhyolite in which Lake Superior agates formed.

There are competing theories on how these agates formed, with the most prominent being that mineral-infused liquids gradually seeped into the air pockets and hardened. Over millions of years, weathering freed many of these agate nodules from their host rock, and ice age glaciers and fast-flowing rivers distributed them widely throughout the Upper Midwest. Even today, agates continue to be moved and exposed by natural forces, such as wave action, ice-sheet formation, and erosion and deposition along rivers and streams. Human activities, such as farming and sand and gravel mining, expose previously hidden lakers as well.

Compared to other types of agates in this book, high-quality Lake Superior agates are still abundant. But just as with other gemstones, finding good and accessible hunting venues is far more difficult than in the recent past. For example, almost all commercial sand and gravel mining operations (the most productive of all laker hunting sites) forbid public access. And the north shore of Lake Superior, perhaps the best-known hunting venue, has been relentlessly combed for agates for more than 100 years!

However, many viable hunting locations remain, and people are still finding a large number of premium specimens. In fact, Lake Superior agate hunting has experienced significant growth and resurgence as of this writing. And there is more good news! Hunting for Lake Superior agates is inexpensive, as there is little or no special equipment required. Lake Superior agates do not need to be dug out, mined, or extracted from the host materials in which they formed, sparing the need for specialized equipment or backbreaking labor. Additionally, there is much fun to be had cutting, polishing, and making jewelry from these beautiful gemstones, and the relative cost of equipment for amateur lapidary artists is quite reasonable.

Just as important as knowing where to hunt is knowing exactly what you're hunting for. Lakers come in a dizzying variety of colors, patterns, and types, and you'll need to acquaint yourself with the most common ones. We will also help you learn about the many types of rocks and minerals that can look very similar to lakers; we refer to those as "imposters." Two kinds of rock that are often found along with lakers are basalt and rhyolite—the host materials in which Lake Superior agates formed. If you travel along the north shore of Lake Superior, you will see the massive basalt and rhyolite cliffs and rock outcroppings. These rock layers run up to 18 miles deep beneath the Lake Superior basin.

Hunting for Lake Superior agates in a farm field

The first photo above shows basalt and rhyolite; the dark-gray-colored rocks are primarily basalt, while those with a more brownish or reddish color are mostly rhyolite. The second photo shows an agate still inside the host basalt in which it formed.

# LAKE SUPERIOR AGATE TYPES AND FEATURES

This section provides photographs of the most prominent Lake Superior agate types and features. It can be helpful to acquire representative samples of these, especially in your early days of learning to hunt for Lake Superior agates.

**Agate types:** There is a tremendous diversity of Lake Superior agate types, and there is significant variation within these types. Because of this variability, the beginning agate hunter is well advised to collect and inspect any stone that displays common laker features. This section will introduce you to Lake Superior agate types, explain where they are most commonly found, and provide you with both rough exterior views and with "internal" views that show the most striking features. Keep in mind that while some of the agate types are listed as common or moderately common, this only pertains to how common they are within the total population of Lake Superior agates. Good quality lakers of any type are actually quite rare (although abundant in comparison to the Fairburn agates of South Dakota).

**Agate features:** Because it's common to find agates facedown or covered with dirt or film (thereby obscuring the often-telltale banding), there are several notable features on the exterior of agates that will help you identify them in the rough. The following agate features can occur on and in many agate types: pitting, limonite staining, translucence, waxy glow, geode crystals, amethyst and smoky quartz, quartz, crystal impression, peeling, floating bands, and opalization.

**Additional types not shown:** There are many agate types not shown, either because they are somewhat or very rare or because they are not highly sought-after or valued, including copper inclusion, skip-an-atom, brecciated, disrupted band/hurricane, seam, and Thunder Bay vein-seam.

# Lake Superior Agate Types

**Fortification agate:** The most common type of laker is the fortification agate, which displays concentric banding patterns. These two gems have the signature red-and-white color scheme.

Fortification agates also commonly occur as bands of gray and white, brown and white, blue and white, green and white, and many other color combinations, including a striking black and white.

**Gravitationally banded (or water-level) agates:** These agates feature parallel lines that might have resulted from heavier mineral contents. The first example shows a combination of fortification and gravitational bands.

**Tube agates:** Tubular structures run all the way through these agates. The second example has been "ventifacted"–weathered and worn by wind-blown sand.

**Floating bands:** Bands that "float" within quartz deposits can create a beautiful display because the quartz layers provide additional translucence that can highlight the bands and colors.

**Amethyst-filled agates:** These are one of the rarest and most highly sought-after types of laker. When polished, the well-defined amethyst crystals are especially vibrant and beautiful.

**Moss and plume agates:** While these are sometimes thought of as low-grade types of agates, many specimens are highly detailed and colorful and would be a highlight in any collection.

**Eye agates:** These agates are quite rare, especially when the eye formations are clustered, or if individual eyes are very large. The "eyes" are actually spherical, and they protrude into the agate.

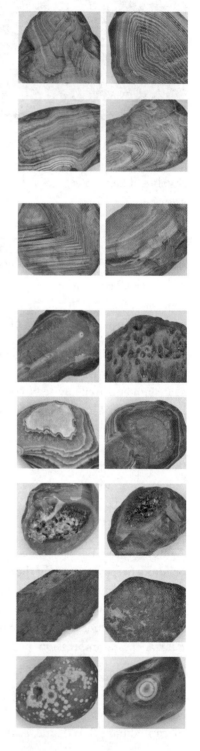

**Paint agates:** "Paints" are also rare and are highly sought-after. They feature vibrant peach and orange colors that are sometimes accompanied by deep browns or a rainbow of red, green, yellow, and blue colors. Paints can also have the most intricately detailed banding patterns, and they polish magnificently.

**Embedded agates:** Agates still in their host rock are wonderful collection pieces that give a glimpse into the complex formation processes that happened millions of years ago.

## Lake Superior Agate Features (for Identification)

**Pitting:** Pitting in the outer husk is the most common feature of lake superior agates. These pits can be large and dimply, fine pinpoints, or well-rounded and spherical. You will learn to recognize these variations as you gain experience.

**Limonite staining:** Limonite is another common and key identification feature for lakers. When you spot that bright-yellow color, pick up the stone and take a closer look. Limonite is only skin deep and often adds to the natural beauty of the stone.

**Colors:** Lakers come in a rainbow of colors, and many agates have their own rainbows. When you see glowing color combinations, it's a good clue.

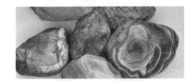

**Translucence:** This is another major identification feature. Sunlight or other strong lighting will make highly translucent agates faintly "glow."

**Waxy luster:** Agates with flat surfaces will generally have a soft or waxy luster. This is true of some imposters too.

**Quartz fill:** While crystalline quartz tends to decrease the beauty and value of agates, sometimes it adds an extra highlight, especially when the quartz crystals are nicely defined.

**Peeling:** Peeled layers are a great way to identify agates, even when they're dirty or if it's cloudy. The peeling also adds to the natural beauty of good-quality agate specimens.

## IMPOSTERS

There are many beautiful and colorful kinds of stones in the Lake Superior agate hunting regions, and many of them have the same kinds of features that help us to identify agates. We like to refer to these look-alikes as "imposters." Here are some of the most common imposters and the features they share with lakers.

**Rainbow (dull-chalky) chalcedony:** Chalcedony has many of the same characteristics as agates, including translucence and bright colors, but it never has well-defined patterns. This type of chalcedony is somewhat less translucent, but the colors will get your attention.

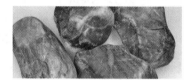

**Bright translucent chalcedony:** The brighter and more translucent varieties of chalcedony sometimes even come with "mock banding" that has to be inspected under magnification to clearly determine whether or not it's an agate.

**Caramel, gray, and white chert:** Like chalcedony, chert shares many of the common characteristics of agates, including banding, pitting, and bright colors. However, chert is opaque, while most agates other than paint agates are translucent.

**Colorful pitted chert:** Chert also comes in more-colorful varieties, with pitting and limonite staining. But chert will never have finely detailed patterns.

**Banded rhyolite:** The bright-orange colors of rhyolite, and occasional external pitting, will catch your eye. Flow-banded rhyolite also has pattern, but it's not as finely detailed as in agates.

**Porphyritic rhyolite:** Porphyritic rhyolite doesn't have a pattern, but it is often pitted and nicely rounded, sometimes with a deep-orange color close to that of agates.

**Quartzite, mica, and feldspar:** Rocks with the vibrant colors of quartzite, mica, and feldspar, including red and white, will catch your eye because of their similarity to agate colors. But they are devoid of pattern. And silver mica flecks don't occur in agates.

**Banded jasper:** The deep-red colors and banding of banded jasper will get your attention, but that banding is never as detailed as in agates. Banded jasper is great for polishing and jewelry-making.

**Mary Ellen jasper:** In addition to jasper's deep-red color, Mary Ellen jasper (or stromatolite jasper) has finely detailed patterns. However, the pattern is not reoccurring or symmetrical as in fortification agates. It is great for jewelry-making.

**Banded flint:** Because banded flint is dull and opaque, you'll learn to distinguish it from agates very quickly. Also, the banding is not nearly as finely detailed.

**Porphyry:** Some porphyry specimens will get your attention because of their vibrant colors and occasional pitting. But they never have finely detailed banding patterns.

**Sandstone:** Sandstone comes in a wonderful variety of colors and patterns. Those with light-red lines will get your attention, but the coarse, sandy texture will tell you they aren't agates.

# LAKE SUPERIOR AGATE PROSPECTING REGIONS

Lake Superior agates can be found across an extremely wide area, but there are regions where your likelihood of finding Lake Superior agates is higher. Each of these provides different hunting "venues" (such as gravel pits, farm fields, or rivers) where good-quality specimens can be found. This map helps you constrain your hunting to areas most likely to be productive.

**Lake Superior Agate Prospecting Regions**

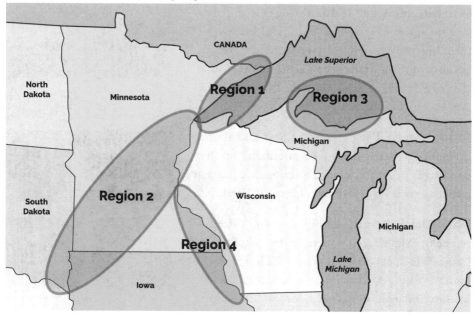

**Region 1**   North shore and western south shore of Lake Superior
**Region 2**   Inland Duluth to northwestern Iowa
**Region 3**   Eastern south shore of Lake Superior
**Region 4**   Mississippi River (from St. Paul, Minnesota, to northwestern Illinois)

Each hunting region provides its own set of venues, in part due to the natural forces that have acted on those agates over the years. The map on the next page depicts some of the Midwest's many glaciation events, helping to illustrate why certain regions have higher concentrations of Lake Superior agates. Material from the Lake Superior basin was moved mostly to the south and west. Agate distribution is erratic because of the succession of glacial lobes that repeatedly advanced and retreated, following a different path and direction each time. Moving water, including rivers and streams, also played a role.

**Direction of Glacial Movement in the Upper Midwest**

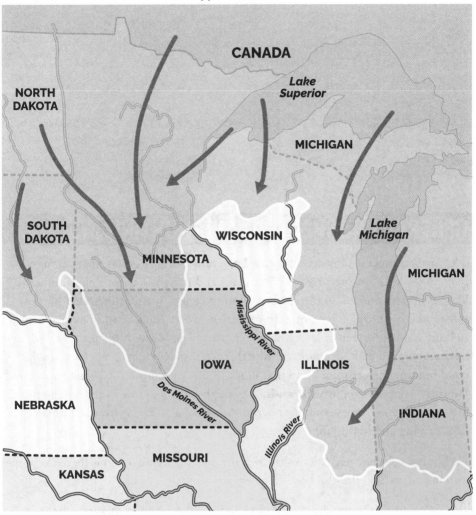

The table that follows addresses the hunting venues within each region and what your odds of good hunting are in each. The table also identifies some agate types that either occur exclusively in that region, or that occur with a much higher frequency than in other regions. For example, eye agates can be found in every region, but I've found them much more frequently along the Mississippi River than within the other hunting venues. And EUP (eastern Upper Peninsula) and copper replacement agates occur exclusively on the eastern Upper Peninsula of Michigan, along the south shore of Lake Superior.

**Odds of Good Hunting at Lake Superior Agate Prospecting Venues**

| Hunting Venue | Region 1 | Region 2 | Region 3 | Region 4 |
| --- | --- | --- | --- | --- |
| Lakeshore | Medium | Low | High | N/A |
| Gravel Pit | High | High | Medium | High |
| Farm Field | Low | High | Low | Low |
| River/stream | Medium | Medium | Low | High |
| Landscaping Rock | Medium | Medium | Medium | Medium |
| Agate Types Exclusive or Highly Likely | Skip-an-atom, Paradise Beach | None | EUP, Keweenaw, copper replacement | Eye |

# GENERAL PROSPECTING AND HUNTING PROCESS

The general process of prospecting for Lake Superior agates has many things in common with prospecting for other gems and minerals. Most important is identifying the areas, and the specific hunting venues within them, that have a substantial quantity of good-quality specimens. Next you'll need to gain approval to hunt and collect, but at least you won't need to go through the process of doing land searches or staking claims. While there are some public lands that provide good hunting opportunities and that don't require specific permissions, most good hunting venues are on private lands. The methods we outline in this chapter will help you narrow your search for good hunting venues, saving yourself unnecessary driving and hiking time.

Each hunting venue necessitates its own prospecting approach, but there are some general things that they all have in common.

- You must determine the ownership and legal status of any land where you hunt for agates. You can't assume that wide-open sections of lakeshore, riverfront, or fields are open for hunting and collecting, even if you regularly see other people hunting there. And the legal status can change, so you need to **verify the status at least annually**.

- If you are given approval to hunt by a private landowner, remember that this approval is only for you. It does not extend to other friends or acquaintances that the landowner hasn't met. So always be sure to identify who you will be hunting with when you talk with the landowner.

- Even if you have obtained approval to hunt on privately owned land, there may be landowners or site operators that don't know that you have received approval from someone else. If someone approaches you and is not aware that you've received permission from someone else, calmly explain the details of who you spoke with. If the person still insists that you leave the property, it's best to comply and then follow up afterwards with the person you first spoke with. For this reason, when someone gives you approval, write down details of the event, such as their name and the date of your conversation.

- Remember that your approval to hunt may come with conditions, such as only hunting farm fields before crops have been planted or after harvest.

- Hunting venues that are widely known and generally accessible can become over-hunted, exhausting the supply of good-quality specimens.

- Because obtaining permission to access private land can be time-consuming, it's good to first judge whether the land may offer a reasonable potential for productive hunting. For example, simply viewing farm fields from the roadside can provide a general sense of the number and types of rocks and minerals present. This usually needs to be done in the spring or fall, when there are no crops growing in the field.

## Safety Factors

Agate hunting in these regions and venues is generally quite safe, but there are several things to be aware of and prepare for. Here is a basic list of safety factors to consider.

- **Weather:** The most significant weather concern is severe thunderstorms, which can produce hail or even tornadoes. It's good to stay vigilant as the day wears on, especially if hunting in remote areas. Extreme heat or cold can be a problem as well. It's easy to let your zeal for finding a prized specimen overtake your natural sense of heat exhaustion or hypothermia. Again, plan ahead and be reasonable about how much time you should spend hunting, based on the conditions.

- **Wildlife:** There are few dangerous or venomous creatures to be concerned with in Lake Superior agate-hunting regions. Wolves, bears, coyotes, and foxes tend to shy away from humans. Moose encounters are possible (but rare) in northern Minnesota, and they can be aggressive toward humans. In general, keep your distance and be prepared to move to a safe place if you see any animals taking an interest in or moving toward you. Venomous snakes can be found in the more southerly portions of Lake Superior agate-hunting regions, such as Iowa and southern Minnesota and Wisconsin, especially near rivers and streams.

- **Climbing and landslides:** Agate hunting on steep hillsides or rock piles, especially at gravel pits and on riverbanks, can result in serious falls. **And sloped or vertical rock, sand, and gravel faces can collapse or cave-in suddenly, releasing tons of material.** This risk is heightened in early spring or after significant rainfalls. Use caution and move slowly; don't let your enthusiasm get in the way of good judgement.

- **Water:** When hunting along rivers and lakeshores, assess risks such as fast-moving currents and heavy, pounding surf. While these conditions can be tempting to ignore because of the possibility that they will provide a lot of fresh, clean rock to hunt in, you must heed your instincts and know your own limitations.

- **Human factors:** Because agate hunting often takes place in more-remote areas, you can be more vulnerable to people that might take advantage of your isolation. It is always best and usually more enjoyable to hunt with a partner. Bring your phone along with you, and in addition, you might decide to carry a portable safety device, such as mace or a whistle.

## LAKESHORES

While the thought of shoreline hunting for Lake Superior agates obviously conjures up images of the Big Lake itself, remember that in the Land of 10,000 Lakes, there are also many smaller lakes with agate-bearing glacial sand and gravel. While these smaller lakes obviously have less of this material, and may have been hunted extensively, they should not be ignored. Also, these smaller lakes are generally more amenable to snorkeling or simply swimming with a face mask.

Don't forget to consider the numerous rivers and streams that feed Lake Superior and other lakes; these venues can be just as productive as hunting on the shore-line itself. These hunting venues are covered later in the chapter.

## Finding Good Hunting Shores

The best shoreline areas for hunting Lake Superior agates have the following characteristics:

- Active surf with minimal natural or man-made "breakers," which substantially reduce wave action
- Large volume of rocks that have been worn smooth by wave action
- Less-than-easy access, such as needing to hike, canoe, or kayak to a site, which will reduce the number of other hunters that you have to compete with

Finding the shoreline areas that meet these requirements involves driving along roads nearest the shoreline and periodically getting out to inspect the shoreline. If there are any access points marked as private or no-trespassing, remember to obtain permission from the landowner before entering.

POOR: Beautiful beach with blue sky and water, but no rocks

POOR: Basalt outcropping and no lake-tumbled rocks for hunting

GOOD: Fair amount of lake-tumbled rock for hunting, but not much wave action to renew things along the shoreline

GOOD: Vigorous wave action and lots of larger lake-tumbled rock; great place for hunting but somewhat risky, with the heavy surf and the steep slope down to the water

EXCELLENT: A protected cove with promising wave-tumbled rock that probably gets renewed frequently; also a relatively secluded location that doesn't get a lot traffic

EXCELLENT: Tons of lake-tumbled rock and a moderately active surf. Perfection!

## Obtaining Approval to Hunt and Collect

- **Public beaches and parks:** Because there are large sections of public land along the north shore of Lake Superior and other inland lakes, it is easy to find sections of the shoreline that are open for hunting. Usually these are designated as public beaches or parks, and most are open for hunting, unless explicitly posted to prohibit hunting and collecting. Keep in mind that these beachfront areas are likely heavily hunted and therefore less likely to produce many good-quality agates. However, your odds are improved if there have been large storms recently, if it is early spring and the ice has just receded, or if you are willing to wade into the water.

- **State parks:** Minnesota State Parks require a daily or annual pass to visit and explore them, and most prohibit collecting any kinds of rocks and minerals. You are free to hunt for them, but you cannot take them home—except in photos, of course. Some people are fine with this experience, equating it to catch-and-release fishing; to them, it's about the thrill of the hunt, and just having their picture taken with a beautiful specimen is sufficient. Michigan's State Parks, on the other hand, generally allow both hunting and collecting, with limitations.

- **Native American reservation lands:** In general, it's best not to hunt on Native American lands unless you are accompanied by a tribal member. Their hunting rules and restrictions aren't always readily available, and there are plenty of other hunting locales to choose from.

- **Privately owned residential or commercial beachfront property:** There are landowners along Lake Superior and other inland lakes that will allow you to hunt for and collect agates on their property, and many of them don't have interest in collecting rocks and minerals themselves. A simple knock on the door, polite greeting, and brief explanation of your interest in rockhounding will often yield consent for you to hunt and collect. If the owners do give you their approval, be sure to ask about any rules they might have and whether you can return anytime.

## The Hunting Experience

In general, hunting on lakeshores can be a serene and even contemplative experience, but it can also be physically and mentally intense if hunting in active surf or when moving stones to see what lies beneath the top layers. As with other hunting venues, we encourage you to prioritize your time among different hunting methods and different sizes of stones. But first, you need to gauge the conditions.

- Is there a good, rolling wave action (not pounding surf with big waves) that is moving a lot of rocks around near the shoreline? If so, this suggests a good opportunity to do some hunting while standing in the water near shore.

- Are there signs of a lot of foot traffic in the rock that is already on shore, indicating the rocks are already well-hunted? If so, it will take some effort to move away the top layers with your feet or possibly a heavy metal rake. You'll need to confine this effort to small and medium rocks that are easy to move.

- If it's sunny, it's helpful to wear polarized sunglasses, especially if hunting at the water's edge or in shallow water near the shore. This will give you a much clearer view of the stones in the water without all the glare of the sun.

We recommend the following lakeshore hunting spots and methods, listed in order of priority.

- **Hunting at the water's edge:** This is usually the most productive because the wave action provides a constant renewal of material for you to inspect. It's best to have a pair of hip waders, or at least sturdy water shoes, so that you can stand where the waves are rolling in. Select a spot where there is a lot of rock, and stand near the water's edge, facing the lake. Let a few sets of waves roll through, and then proceed along the shoreline in 3- to 5-foot increments. In shallow-water areas near shore where the waves aren't too strong, you can use a "bucket scope," which is simply a 5-gallon bucket with the bottom cut out and replaced by a piece of sturdy plexiglass. Another nice tool for hunting in water is a "treasure scoop," which has a metal claw and scoop on a long aluminum or stainless steel shaft for scooping up rocks in lakes and rivers. Some rock shops sell treasure scoops and bucket scopes.

- **Hunting rocks already on the shore:** This can be very productive, especially if you're the first on the scene after a strong storm. Work the entire beachfront, from the waterline to as far back as it appears that waves deposited new rocks. Start with the larger rocks in the back, exploiting the opportunity to find large agates. Even if people have been there before you, you can still search in a methodical grid pattern. When looking through larger rocks, train yourself to look through and beneath the top layer to try to spot agate features that are only barely visible. Finally, you can select a given stretch of beach and manually move rocks off the surface layer to expose rocks beneath. For rocks bigger than 3 to 5 inches in diameter, you'll probably need to take a seat and move them one by one, tossing them a safe distance away. When looking through smaller rocks, sweep layers of rock away with your feet, or by hand if sitting down. It's really peaceful sitting and working through small stones and listening to the surf, and you can keep scooting along the shoreline as you comb through the material within your reach.

- **Snorkeling and scuba diving:** These are two great ways to see rocks that haven't been actively hunted. Make sure that you are respectful of sharp rocks, and beware of rough surf that can force you onto unforgiving rock surfaces.

- **Canoeing and kayaking:** These are great ways to access more-remote hunting spots, such as shallow offshore areas amenable to wading, snorkeling, or using a bucket scope.

Lakeshore agate hunters can suffer from visual overload, similar to hunting on large piles of washed rock at gravel pits. Your best bet is to "park it" and get up-close and personal with the stones.

But even though you are close up, you'll still need to look for the smallest of clues. Unlike rough agates found at gravel pits and in farm fields, lake-tumbled agates have had many of their identifying features worn away, such as limonite staining, pitting, or conchoidal fractures.

Watch for rocks with color variations that make them stand out from the other stones, and flip them over.

Watch for the telltale deep-red-and-white color combination that is a signature of Lake Superior agates.

Translucence and rainbow color combinations are great cues to pick stones up for a closer look.

In the water, agate banding is highly visible. Standing in shallow water and letting the waves tumble and roll the stones is a great way to relax and look for colorful banding. You'll need to move quickly if you see something promising because the next wave might roll that stone over, hiding its identifying features.

## GRAVEL PITS

### Finding the Gravel Pits

Maps created by the Minnesota DNR's Aggregate Resource Mapping Program greatly facilitate prospecting. These online maps show areas where there is a high concentration of glacial till (sand and gravel that was moved and deposited by glacial activities). This will help you hone in on possible hunting locations. In areas that were visited by glaciers from the Lake Superior basin, these gravel pits typically contain Lake Superior till. While the maps specifically identify sand and gravel pits, they are also useful as a guide for other hunting venues; where you find Lake Superior gravel, you will also likely find farm fields with agates.

Satellite images are a wonderful tool for finding gravel pits. There are many satellite imagery providers available, such as Google Earth or the USGS National Map. Start by looking for odd-shaped light-colored tracts of land, and then zoom in to look for further signs that it's not just farmland, such as sand and gravel piles, pools of water, and even mining equipment. The close-up image on page 28 shows the long conveyers used to move and sort material.

Keep in mind that satellite views will reveal both active sand and gravel mining operations and ones that are recently inactive, plus the images could be as much as 3 years out of date, but they are still a worthwhile starting point. It's helpful to purchase detailed county-by-county road map books and then use the aggregate maps to highlight the areas of higher sand and gravel concentrations and gravel pits.

Using satellite imagery to find gravel pits    *Map services and data available from USGS, Nat. Geospatial Program*

And now it's time to get in the car and head out to do some prospecting! When you discover viable hunting sites, and make contact with property owners and site operators, you can write the details in the county map book itself or in a corresponding notepad.

## Obtaining Approval to Hunt and Collect

**Commercial sand and gravel pits:** These are the most productive sites for hunting and collecting Lake Superior agates, due to their size and activities. They excavate gravel, creating large walls of sand and gravel that are subject to erosion from rain events, and they sort the gravel (by size) and wash it. However, and this is a BIG HOWEVER, due to insurance provisions and safety regulations, they often do not allow any non-company personnel on their premises for any reason.

Many of these gravel pits are patrolled during off-hours by either company personnel or police, with trespassers being arrested and fined for entering the property. But this does not mean you should give up on gaining approval to hunt in a commercial pit. If you find a gravel pit that you want to hunt and collect in, there are several ways you can approach things.

The first thing you will need is a talking script, which you can adapt for use in requesting access to farm fields, residential lakeshore properties, landscaping businesses, and other private properties. Following is the core script for you to start with; adapt it as you see fit, as you gain experience.

- Introduce yourself and say where you are from.

- If the person you are speaking with is open to it, engage in some small talk to break the ice.

- Explain that you are an avid rock hunter and you like to hunt for Lake Superior agates.

- Let them know if you have been granted access to hunt at other gravel pits, and if so, that you always comply with any rules, such as not being on premises when the crew is working.

- Ask for the company's policy or the name and contact information of someone you can speak with.

- If at any point in time you are given a firm "no," it's best to politely accept and end the conversation.

- If you are given approval, you should ask for the name of the person giving the approval and write it down, along with the date; you should also ask whether there are any rules or restrictions they want you to follow and then document those as well.

- Thank people for their time; it reflects well on rock and mineral enthusiasts.

- You can offer to provide a signed premises liability disclaimer, which states that you will not sue the operator or property owner under any circumstances; you can find examples of these on the internet and adapt them to your specific situation.

## Approaches for Requesting and Obtaining Approval

- The best approach is to find out whether you have a connection to anyone that works at the company. Think about it like job networking—if the company has a policy against agate hunting, someone that knows you might be able to get you an exception.

- The second-best method is to approach the work crew and ask if there is a foreman that you can talk to. The foreman or manager will usually be able to give you a firm yes or no on the spot, and you should never challenge their decision. You might be pleasantly surprised when after politely accepting a "no," they volunteer some advice on other sites that might allow hunting, or even offer you some leeway in the company's policy.

- Many sand and gravel mining operations take place on leased land. In these cases, it might be possible to obtain permission from the landowner, but the company operating in the pit still has the authority to deny you hunting access while they have an active lease. To find out who owns the land, you can look up properties in county records, you can stop at nearby houses to ask who owns the land, and you can ask the pit operators.

- If you don't know anyone at the company operating the gravel pit, you can call the company office. This should be your last resort, as you are almost certain to get the standard company policy recited to you, and then you are on record as having been told "no." There are some small and medium-size companies that are more flexible, but the very large companies almost always forbid non-company personnel on their active sites.

**County gravel pits:** These pits tend to be much more flexible, but it is still best to use the same approaches as with private pits. The only difference is that you will be talking with someone in a county administration office instead of a company office.

**Privately owned and operated gravel pits:** These also tend to be more flexible. For these it is simply a matter of tracking down the landowner, as we've previously described, and then following the standard talking script once you have made contact.

**Abandoned and inactive gravel pits:** Inactive pits can be quite productive for many years after sand and gravel mining operations have stopped. In fact, the largest Lake Superior agate that I ever found (nearly 3 pounds!) was discovered in a pit that had been defunct for several years. As with active pits, locate the landowner and follow the talking script.

## The Hunting Experience

Gravel pits provide the greatest range of hunting methods. Most people think of gravel pit hunting as simply climbing on rock piles, but there are several hunting options within most pits. None of these methods are better than another. Deciding which to use comes down to a person's hunting preferences and abilities, and to the "condition" of each one of these options, such as whether there is fresh, clean rock or whether it has been heavily picked over. The best advice is to follow the sun, which means to hunt in areas where there is good sunlight and move throughout the day as needed. But should you happen to enter a pit that has a pile of newly sorted large rocks, then by all means make this your priority!

- Rock piles provide the greatest concentration of rock and therefore the greatest opportunities for finding agates. The best rock piles have been sorted by size, washed by rain or machine spray washing, have a low ratio of crushed rock pieces to whole rocks, and show no evidence of other hunters climbing on the piles. Rocks are typically sorted into these size ranges: $\frac{1}{2}$ to 1 inch, 1 to 3 inches, and greater than 3 inches. Start with the largest rock first to optimize your chances of finding larger agates, but reserve some of your time for the smaller rocks because your odds of finding good-quality agates go up as size goes down. There are simply more small agates than very large agates.

- After selecting a rock pile, first slowly walk the perimeter of the pile without stepping on the pile itself. You'll want to inspect the surface layer of rocks, and stepping on the pile might cause a cascade of rocks, burying the top rocks that you haven't looked at yet. Take your time because your eyes and brain are processing thousands of micro-images. Even as a seasoned hunter, I have failed to follow my own advice, only to have a fellow hunter come after me and scoop up a prized agate. After walking the perimeter, you can start to step onto the pile, moving around and up in a slight ascending spiral. I recommend stepping in places that allow you to distribute your weight carefully to reduce large cascades of rock. The cascades will eventually happen, but the higher you can get up the pile without disturbing the surface layer, the better your chances. When you've made it to the top of the pile, you should descend to the bottom and then begin to move rock deliberately. Use raking motions with your boots

to cause rocks to slide down the pile. This will give you a new layer of rock to observe each time you go around. Note that the larger rocks generally settle to the bottom, so each time down, be sure to pay close attention to those that have rolled farther down the pile.

**Be especially cautious when climbing on piles of large rocks**, which tend to move individually and suddenly, unlike the "incremental" give or sliding of small rocks. This means it's easy to lose your footing and take a hard tumble. Plant your feet carefully, and move around the pile slowly. Take time to look at rocks beneath the surface layer. This is easier with larger rocks because of the larger gaps between them. While photographing for this book, we were talking about this technique and then scored a 1.5-pound beauty. This agate has about a $400 value, but of course, it will stay in this young man's collection his whole life!

- Sand and gravel "walls" line active gravel pits. The virgin material being mined here has been untouched since the receding glaciers deposited it many thousands of years ago. For this reason, many experienced hunters make this their first stop of the day, especially when there has been a hard rain to wash the newly exposed rocks. **Keep in mind that these sand and gravel walls call for extreme caution due to the risk of collapse and falling rocks.** As with rock piles, start by working at the bottom. If you notice rows of footsteps, try to walk a path in between sets of footsteps, giving yourself a different point of view that might help you see agates that the previous hunter missed. Walk laterally along the entire section of the wall, then move up about 6 feet and walk laterally in the opposite direction, repeating until you've either reached the top, or the angle of incline is

too steep to go up another level. Do not be discouraged if you see another set of footprints because every hunter, no matter how experienced, will miss things. If you see lots of fresh footprints, it's probably best to check out another area within the gravel pit.

- The "floor" of gravel pits is often overlooked because of the assumption that all of that rock has been hunted many times before. The truth is that with all of the equipment hauling sand and gravel around, periodic erosion caused by heavy rains, and cleaning of the rocks by rain, you can still find high-quality specimens in an area that hasn't been mined for years! And it's very easy hunting, plus it's less likely to be shaded from the sun. For best success, choose an area with a lot of gravel, and walk it methodically in a grid pattern.

- Newly landscaped areas around the gravel pits are prized just as much as fresh gravel walls. A top layer of soil, grass, and trees is removed to expose the rich layers of glacial sand and gravel. These areas will usually have a gentler slope, and after being rained on, they become fabulous exposures of clean rocks that are easy to hunt on. It's best to walk laterally across such slopes rather than bottom to top because it's a bit more efficient and less strenuous. However, the very best results come from first walking back and forth laterally as you go up the slope, and then walking the runoff valleys, where larger amounts of rock accumulate and roll down the slope.

## FARM FIELDS

### Finding Good Farm Fields

DNR aggregate maps (see page 27) are a wonderful resource for locating farm fields with an abundance of glacial sand and gravel that could contain agates. This is also true for the satellite imagery approach to finding gravel pits (see page 27). There is almost always a wide area around the actual pits that contains rocks and gravel. Drive to where the maps show these areas, and begin to observe the farm fields. You might wonder whether farm fields still have a good supply of agates after many years of hunting (and it's hard to know which fields have been actively hunted in the past), but farming practices do continue to bring new rocks to the surface. I've found many premium agates in fields that I've hunted in for more than 10 years!

Not much rock

Loaded

Clean rock and some crop residue

Too much crop residue

When you spot a rocky field, stop to take a closer look. If it's after harvest, crop residue can cover a lot of the rocks, but that doesn't necessarily mean that all of the rocks are covered or that hunting the field wouldn't be productive. If the field looks like a good candidate for hunting, it's time to find the landowner and try to obtain permission.

These days, farmers may own land in multiple locations, so they may live a distance from some of their fields, and some farmland may belong to an absentee landowner who lives in another city or even state. However, nearby property owners can often point out who owns the land, where they live, or how to contact them. But if this doesn't work, you can always access public records, either at local county offices, online, or through handy smartphone apps that show property lines and landowners.

## Obtaining Approval to Hunt and Collect

Obtaining access to hunt in farm fields is refreshingly relaxed and simple compared to gravel pits. In fact, most farmers are friendly and happy to have a short conversation about our hobby. But there is a chance they may say "no," and that must be respected. If they have rules for hunting and collecting on their property, follow them. And always remember that any approval they have given you does not automatically extend to all of your friends and family. Make sure to ask these things specifically, and check back in with them periodically. You may want to ask the landowners if they hunt for agates themselves, and if so, if they have any agates they would like to show off or sell. If you are interested in purchasing any agates, offer a fair price, such as about 60% of what a retail shop might charge.

## The Hunting Experience

Farm field hunting is perhaps one of the most casual rockhounding experiences you'll ever find. You are almost always hunting on flat or slightly rolling land. And while you'll encounter muddy conditions at times, the worst that can happen is the mud sucks your boot(s) off and you have some cleanup once you get home. But the process of methodically walking rows in a field allows plenty of time for listening to music, self-reflection, and just enjoying the outdoors, including any birds or other animals that might happen by. It's great exercise as well.

The hunting process itself is quite simple—just walk back and forth across the field using visible tillage lines, wheel tracks, or crop rows as markers. If crops have already been planted and you've been allowed to hunt after planting, be sure not to step on the growing plants. You often may not have time to walk all of the acres available to you, so focus on walking areas with a lot of exposed rocks.

Choose a row to walk down, and look at rocks in that row and the rows immediately to the right and left of it. Once you get to a spot without much surface rock (or the end of the field), move over three rows, as depicted below, with each **red row** representing the rows you'll be walking down. With this method, you only observe each row once. If you want to be more thorough, such as in a very rocky area, you can shift one row each time, and this way you will see each row three times, including from more than one direction. Once you've looked through all the rocks in one area, move to another rocky part of the field and begin again.

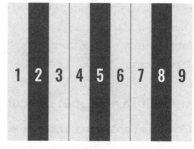

At some point, you may notice piles of rocks outside the perimeter of a field. Most farms with rocky soil have these rock piles, the result of decades of removing rocks from the field. Large rocks in farm fields present a hazard to farm machinery. While some older piles (indicated by moss and lichen growth) might have been scouted previously for agates, it's worth your time to at least browse the piles, especially if it looks like more rocks have been added recently.

## RIVERS AND STREAMS

For beginning and even experienced agate hunters, your best chances of success will be on sand and gravel bars and on the banks lining the river or stream. It is exceedingly difficult to spot an agate in rolling and rippling water, and the water is often muddy or cloudy, even if walking upstream; therefore we recommend onshore hunting exclusively. Because there are usually a limited number of public access points, a canoe or kayak will help you cover more of the waterway. Rivers and streams can be subject to significant erosion from heavy rains and snowmelt, resulting in significant turnover of the rocks they hold. This makes them fruitful, even if often overlooked, hunting opportunities.

### Finding Good River Shores

Some notable places to start your search are the St. Croix, Minnesota, and Mississippi Rivers, and the feeder streams along the north shore of Lake Superior. All other rivers and streams within the hunting ranges depicted on the regional maps are also worth checking, and considering that rivers are constantly moving things downstream, these waterways may contain agates well beyond the noted ranges. You can scout out sand and gravel bars using satellite imagery, or you can do the drive-around method if you live close to any larger rivers and streams. You can use a DNR map to find public access points to bodies of water. Here is an example link:

https://files.dnr.state.mn.us/maps/water_access/counties/benton_sherburne.pdf

Poor: Muddy water and no sign of gravel bars with tumbled stones

Poor: Muddy water that is choked with leaves and debris

Poor: High rapids and large basalt boulders and chunks; no gravel bars of tumbled rock

Good: Modest amount of tumbled rocks with relatively calm water and a steep bank, which is a source of new rock to erode down into the stream

## Obtaining Approval to Hunt and Collect

Observe the following restrictions when hunting and collecting:

- Minnesota state parks and Native American reservation lands are off-limits for hunting and collecting.

- Hunting and collecting are allowed along larger rivers in Minnesota, such as the Mississippi, Minnesota, and St. Croix Rivers, except within state park boundaries. The specific law states that: When a water basin or watercourse is "navigable," the State of Minnesota owns the bed below the natural ordinary low water level. ("Navigable" usually means that the river could be used for commercial transportation.)

- You must obtain approval to hunt on shorelines in front of private properties along smaller streams that are non-navigable. We strongly recommend asking property owners on larger navigable rivers, too, as a matter of courtesy. Here is a good reference article:

  https://files.dnr.state.mn.us/publications/waters/Pardon_Me_Myth.pdf

## The Hunting Experience

River shore hunting is somewhat comparable to hunting in gravel pits. Specifically, the riverbanks are similar to what we call "sand and gravel walls" within a gravel pit, and they should be hunted in the same way. This means working the bottom of a section of the riverbank and then moving up the wall in 5- to 6-foot increments, walking laterally at the same "height" along the same section until you've reached the top. Make sure to focus your time and effort on sections of embankment that have a lot of surface rock. In addition, the sand and gravel bars should be hunted in a similar fashion to gravel pit "floors." This means you should methodically work a grid pattern to make sure you cover the space thoroughly. Below are a few additional tips and suggestions.

- Before heading out, consider whether any recent rains or snowmelt might have resulted in dangerous river conditions, especially if you'll be using a canoe or kayak.

- If canoeing or kayaking, base your trip duration on river conditions, your skill level, and the time you plan to spend hunting and collecting.

- Hunting spots farther from an access point are less likely to be overhunted.

- Hunting closer to the water is best because those stones have usually been deposited, or at least turned over, most recently.

- If there are feeder streams, take the time to work these, as well, provided they are within allowed public lands; in general, you might work them away from the river about 100 yards, or as far as there is abundant rock.

- If there has been recent heavy rain or flooding, your chances are greatly improved, even close to access points, but make sure the river conditions are safe for your skill level and comfort.

- Use a canoe, kayak, or raft paddle to splash water onto rocks near the shoreline. Getting the stones wet highlights color and patterns. Working in teams is best, with one person splashing the rocks and one or more people inspecting them as you work your way down the shore.

# URBAN PROSPECTING: LANDSCAPING AND ROOFING ROCK

You might wonder whether this venue and method of hunting for agates is worthwhile. It is! Since getting into commercial gravel mining operations is quite difficult, access to freshly mined and washed rock can only be done by finding the gravel after it has left the mining sites. Countless premium and highly valuable agates have been found in landscaping and roofing rock. However, by law you must ask permission from the property owners before hunting, or they can have you ticketed and fined. Of course, being a patron of a given restaurant or retail store goes a long way in getting this permission. Another benefit of urban prospecting and hunting is direct vehicle access and not much physical exertion required.

## Finding Good Urban Rock

Finding promising landscaping and roofing rock is done through a process called "urban prospecting." Agate hunters who focus on this method learn how to find newly placed rock, which offers a greater probability of finding quality agates than rock that has been searched many times. This typically means keeping track of new construction that might use rock for landscaping or roofing.

Some information can be obtained from publicly available construction permits, but because of unpredictable building schedules and progress, the best bet is simply driving in search of construction sites. Once work has begun, it's a matter of doing a periodic drive-by. If you keep a map of active construction sites, you can optimize your time by

having a route that you drive once or twice per week. Additionally, you can stop and chat with construction workers to find out if and when they'll be using rock for either roofing or landscaping. And buying the work crew a dozen doughnuts just might help your chances of being the first on scene when a large dump truck of fresh rock shows up!

Residential landscaping businesses are another great place to access landscaping gravel. These businesses often have large piles of rock of various sizes for sale. If you are a customer, you might have better luck getting approval to periodically stop by and hunt for agates.

While we've focused more on finding newly delivered gravel, that doesn't mean you should ignore established buildings (commercial or residential). That rock may never have been thoroughly searched by an experienced agate hunter, or it might have recently been rained on or turned over, exposing the face or other features of an agate. Many great agates have been found at long-established housing and business locations.

Always ask for permission to hunt for agates in roofing or landscape rock. Make sure to properly introduce yourself and ask about any restrictions they have, such as where or when you can hunt. At new construction sites, it's best to talk to the crew foreman, and at established buildings or landscaping businesses, seek out the owner or manager.

## The Hunting Experience

Hunting in landscaping and roofing rock is much like the experience at a commercial sand and gravel pit. You will be looking at a large volume of cleaned and sorted rock, truly an agate hunters dream come true! We offer the following tips.

- An extra dose of patience goes a long way—because there is so much rock available to look at, it's easy to lose focus and move too quickly. Instead, stand stationary for 10 to 30 seconds at a time, carefully surveying the rock within a given "vision frame" (such as a 7x7-foot square), and then move to the next "vision frame." If you are hunting on all fours, it will naturally slow your movement.

- If the landscaping rock is in a pile, ask if you can climb on the pile and move rock around. If so, make sure that you've thoroughly inspected the top layer of rock first.

Here is a terrific urban hunting spot with rock that looks lightly trodden, if at all, other than the landscaping crew of course. Also, there are not a lot of weeds or other debris, so this gravel is probably relatively fresh.

- If the rock has already been spread out on the ground, make sure to not only inspect the top layer of rock, but to also look through and beneath the top layer, especially if the rock has been there awhile. Use your feet to gently rake away and turn over the top layer of rock, but be sure that you always leave things well-groomed and looking nice, so the property owners aren't left with that chore after you've finished.

Get low to see the rocks better. Wearing a brimmed hat and avoiding sunglasses gives clear visuals without color distortion.

A hint of the traditional deep-red color and some waxy glow yields a pretty red-and-white.

Limonite staining on this one is a sure giveaway. Here is a nice opalization overlay and shimmering white bands in a deep-gray background.

Limonite plus pitting makes this one a sure agate. How many people walked past this beauty on their way to work?

Here's a nice bin of uncrushed rock fresh from the gravel pit. It's a little bit dirty, but with full sun, things will still pop out. It has a nice mix of sizes too!

Peeling is a great feature to spot when hunting in dirty rock. Here's a very sweet "potato!"

The deep-red color glows on this beauty, with peeled tubes and bright red-and-white banding. Not too bad for some "dirty picking."

Up on the rooftop, it's great to know someone that does HVAC work! Of course, getting the property owner's permission is called for as well.

It's almost impossible to miss the vibrant peach-orange color of this pretty little paint agate.

## TOOLS AND EQUIPMENT

Luckily, Lake Superior agate hunters need little in the way of tools or equipment, and most of what they do need are everyday household items.

### General Tools and Equipment

- Reliable cellphone and service plan within your hunting range
- Sturdy and comfortable hiking boots
- First aid kit
- Large spray bottle and an extra gallon or two of water

- Heavy-duty collecting pouch or knapsack
- Drinking water and nourishing snack foods
- Insect repellent
- Sunscreen
- Sun visor or hat
- Tall rubber boots or water shoes if you'll be crossing or hunting in water
- Small canoe or raft paddle for splashing water onto rocks along shorelines

## Specialty Tools and Equipment

- **Polarized sunglasses, or polarized or non-tinted prescription eyeglasses if you wear them:** Regular sunglasses tend to reduce your ability to see color variations in agates. Polarized sunglasses are great for reducing glare when hunting in or near the water's edge.

- **5–10x magnifier:** Carson MiniBrite ($11) is one good model. These are a must for inspection and identification.

- **Treasure scoop:** For scooping stones out of deep water ($52). https://kingsleynorth.com/treasure-scoop-42-inch.html

# REFERENCES AND RESOURCES

## Books

- Lynch, Dan R., and Bob Lynch. *Agates of Lake Superior: Stunning Varieties and How They Are Formed.* Adventure Publications, 2012.
- Magnuson, Jim. *Agate Hunting Made Easy.* Adventure Publications, 2012.
- Magnuson, Jim. *Lake Superior Agates: Identify Agates and Imposters!* Adventure Publications, 2013

## Facebook Groups

- Lake Superior Agate Collectors www.facebook.com/groups/61978165391
- Great Lakes Rocks & Minerals www.facebook.com/groups/106675549490547

## Rock and Lapidary Shops

- Minnesota Lapidary Supply, Princeton, MN lapidarysupplies.com
- Kingsley North, Norway, MI kingsleynorth.com

- The Gem Shop, Cedarburg, WI
- Agate City, Two Harbors, MN
  www.agatecity.com

## Rock and Mineral Clubs

- Minnesota Mineral Club, St. Paul, MN
  minnesotamineralclub.org
- Cuyuna Rock, Gem & Mineral Society, Brainerd, MN
  cuyunarockclub.org
- Coulee Rock Club, La Crosse, WI
  www.facebook.com/The-Coulee-Rock-Club-182345351787782
- Carlton County Gem & Mineral Club, Cloquet, MN
  www.facebook.com/groups/891164997610511
- Heart of Wisconsin Gem & Mineral Society, Stevens Point, WI
  www.heartofwisconsinrocks.com
- Anoka County Gem & Mineral Club, Anoka, MN
  www.facebook.com/AnokaCountyGemMineralClub
- Chippewa Valley Gem & Mineral Society, Chippewa Falls, WI
  www.facebook.com/groups/CVGMS

## Websites and Reference

- Aggregate Mapping for MN Counties
  www.dnr.state.mn.us/lands_minerals/aggregate_maps/index.html

  www.dnr.state.mn.us/lands_minerals/aggregate_maps/completed/index.html

# FLUORESCENT SODALITE

Of all the wonderful gems and minerals in this book, perhaps none has captured our imagination quite like the fluorescent mineral sodalite. Maybe it's because it's something of a "new kid on the block," but I suspect it has more to do with the hunting experience itself. It's an adventure, hunting for treasures in the dark with ultraviolet (UV) flashlights, yet at the same time it's a peaceful and even meditative experience, walking the shorelines of Lake Superior and hearing the rolling waves. It can also be a wonderful family experience for all ages, with children, parents, grandparents, and friends. But really, what could be more cool than rocks that glow in the dark?!

So what makes fluorescent sodalite-bearing stones "new?" They've recently come to widespread popularity under the trademarked name "Yooperlite®"–from "Yooper" (a resident of the Upper Peninsula—or "UP"–of Michigan, where these stones are most frequently found) and "lite" (which refers to its flourescence). These rocks are mostly syenite, a type of igneous stone that is similar to granite but that lacks granite's silica content, but they also include the fluorescent mineral sodalite.

Because they are found along the southern shores of Lake Superior, they have an incredibly smooth wave-tumbled finish. This means that in their natural or "as found" state they are ready for display with no lapidary work required. However, many lapidary artists have fashioned them into necklaces, pyramids, spheres, skulls, and a variety of other shapes and configurations.

## IMPOSTERS

The only way that you can reliably identify fluorescent sodalite-bearing stones is with a UV light in low light or complete darkness, as all of their imposters look comparable in standard light: speckled and with similar color shading. Think of the UV light as a visual metal detector. This is similar to the way a metal detector will detect the metal in a copper replacement agate, distinguishing it from green-stone and chloride, which can look identical in their rough nodular form.

Diabase
Fluorescent Sodalite
Granite
Gabbro

| Rock/Mineral | Visual Characteristics |
|---|---|
| Granite | It comes in many color variations that can often be identical to syenite. The more vibrantly colored stones can be ruled out. |
| Gabbro | It's usually a darker-gray color, along with lighter-colored material, which makes it possible to visually identify, but some lighter-colored specimens are harder to differentiate from syenite. |
| Diabase | Like gabbro, it's typically a darker-colored gray, but sometimes the dull-white crystal inclusions are very small, making it appear similar to syenite. |

# FLUORESCENT SODALITE PROSPECTING REGIONS

The map below shows where fluorescent sodalite-bearing syenite rocks are actively hunted and found. It is believed that the source material originated near Marathon, Ontario, on the north shore of Lake Superior, and it was brought south by glacial events. Due to the paths taken by various glaciers, sodalite is much more abundant in Region 1. In Region 2, the south shore of Lake Superior holds more sodalite than the north shore.

**When hunting and collecting on public land, it's up to you to know the laws pertaining to the jurisdiction you're in.** To start with, it's illegal to remove rocks and minerals from most state lands in Minnesota and Wisconsin, and the same is true for national parks and lakeshores. In Michigan, the amount of rocks and minerals (other than gold-bearing—that has its own rules) and invertebrate fossils that can be taken from state lands is limited to a total of 25 pounds per person per year. And if hunting on private land, be sure to gain proper authorization. We provide some helpful suggestions in this regard in the Lake Superior Agates chapter (see page 28).

**Fluorescent Sodalite Prospecting Regions**

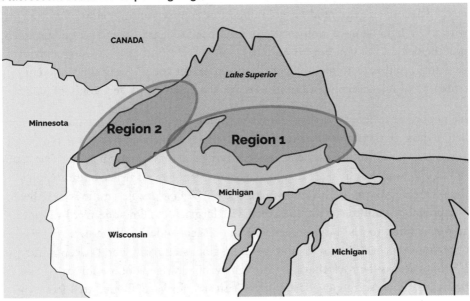

# GENERAL PROSPECTING AND HUNTING PROCESS

Hunting for fluorescent sodalite can be done on lakeshores, in landscaping rock, at gravel pits, and even in rocky farm fields. We're going to focus primarily on lakeshore and landscaping rock. The hunting process in these venues is nearly identical—hunting in large volumes of clean and smooth rock. You won't be faced with climbing, digging, rock breaking, or any arduous hiking.

A good UV flashlight is the essential tool for finding fluorescent sodalite, just as metal detectors are essential for gold nugget or copper hunting. However, working with a UV light is much simpler; there is no need to learn how to set up and interpret the device. All you have is an on-and-off switch! But, as with using a metal detector, you'll need to methodically cover a "target zone," using slow and deliberate side-to-side sweeping motions to cover the area. Think "economy of motion."

It's important to scout out your hunting locations in daylight, at least an hour before dark. This enables you to look around and make a plan to cover the area you want to hunt in; it also helps in identifying safety hazards and orienting yourself to your surroundings. If there have been recent storms or ice-out to refresh the rock along the shoreline and you're one of the first people on the scene, then you probably want to start in the areas with larger rock. One doesn't always get an opportunity to find large stones with fluorescent sodalite. Wherever you start, once you've picked out a section to work in, stop, stand still, and "sweep" your UV light across the rock that's within your visible range, looking for any rocks that give a fluorescent glow. Usually you can step forward about 3 to 4 feet each time and then "sweep" the next set of rocks.

By now you've hopefully gathered that you'll be stopping and starting rather than walking along at a slow and steady pace. Later in this chapter we'll also talk about stationary hunting (sitting) and hunting at the water's edge.

It's a good idea to purchase or borrow one or more fluorescent sodalite specimens to practice learning how to spot them. They are also good for testing your flashlight and its batteries before going out hunting. In fact, bring a spare set of batteries, because the last thing you want to happen when you are having success is to have your flashlight go dead!

## Safety Factors

Waves and weather are two safety factors you need to consider. The shores of Lake Superior can become dangerous very quickly, so keep an eye on changing weather conditions, and stay well clear of the shoreline when there is active surf, especially if there are large, jagged rock formations in the area.

## UV Flashight Options

There are two main types of UV flashlights—filtered and unfiltered. The filtered type provides light with less "noise" or distraction, and it focuses its light more narrowly, so fluorescent material tends to stand out more from the surrounding items. You'll pay a considerable premium for filtered UV flashlights, but in our side-by-side review, the unfiltered flashlight produced results that were almost comparable in both darkness and partial-light conditions. Either way, you won't find yourself spending a fortune to acquire a good-quality light. Page 57 features a model of each type that is worth consideration. If you are going out hunting with multiple people, why not get one or two of each.

## PROCESS DETAILS

Fluorescent sodalite prospecting is definitely all about lighting, and as with anything fluorescent, the darker the area you're in, the more intense you'll find the fluorescent glow. So obviously this means that night hunting is the best and hunting in full sunlight is a waste of time. But in between these two extremes, there is a range of visibility as shown in the photos on pages 54–55. You can see that fluorescent sodalite hunting is possible in daylight hours, given the right conditions and using the right techniques, such as sitting or crouching to get closer to the rocks. Water affects the UV light as well; nighttime hunting for submerged fluorescent sodalite will diminish the fluorescent light intensity by 10–20% in water up to a foot in depth.

We strongly recommend bringing a good standard flashlight for finding your way around and returning safely to "home base." Make sure to identify landmarks that will lead you back to where you started, and periodically make note of additional landmarks as you continue your hunt. Some people stick glow sticks in the ground as they go, marking their path. These can also come in handy for keeping track of what areas you've already covered on larger expanses of beach or landscaping rock.

Here are tips for various lighting situations. Note that in all of these scenarios, it's often worthwhile to move away top layers of rock with your hands or feet, especially if you think that other sodalite hunters have already covered the same area.

Filtered (left) and unfiltered (right) UV in full sunlight at close range: no visible fluorescence

Filtered UV in lightly overcast sunlight at close range: fluorescent light intensity is low, up to a distance of 1 to 3 feet.

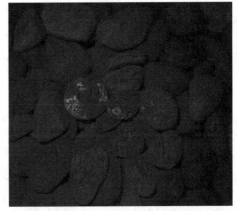

Filtered and unfiltered UV in heavily overcast sunlight at 4 feet from flashlight to stones: fluorescent light intensity is good up to a distance of 3 to 6 feet.

Filtered and unfiltered UV at dusk at 8 feet: fluorescent light intensity is good up to a distance of 6 to 10 feet.

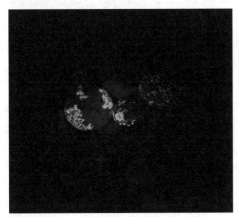

Filtered and unfiltered UV at night at 10 feet: fluorescent light intensity is excellent up to a distance of 8 to 12 feet.

# HUNTING MODES AND SCENARIOS

**Walking the beach at night–on shore:** Arrive at your destination at least an hour before dark to assess hunting and safety conditions and to make and map out your plan and coverage priorities. This also gives you time to visually orient yourself to any landmarks, ensuring you can find your way back quickly in case of emergency or weather. Hold your flashlight at chest or head level to increase the amount of ground that the light covers, 3 to 5 feet in front of your feet.

**Walking the beach at night–at the waterline or in shallow water:** Hunting along the waterline can be very rewarding, but be sure to carefully assess the size and strength of the waves. If the surf isn't too aggressive, you can stand in the water, up to a foot deep, and watch as the waves roll the rocks around. You can do this for a couple of waves and then move along the waterline.

**Hunting in landscaping rock at night:** This is very similar to walking the beach at night, except that you don't generally need to be concerned about getting lost. It's mostly about using a methodical sequence in hunting the rocks.

**Hunting when heavily overcast, or at dawn or dusk:** When hunting in partial daylight, shorten the distance between your flashlight and the rocks. You'll need to do more crouching, holding the flashlight at about at waist level and focusing it on rocks 1 to 3 feet from your feet.

**Hunting when lightly overcast, or in early morning or late evening:** When hunting in lightly overcast conditions, sit, crouch, or crawl along the rocks. You'll need to position the flashlight 6 to 12 inches from the rocks to get visible fluorescence. Shade the area you're looking at with your body or some other light barrier, like a towel or a piece of cardboard.

# TOOLS AND EQUIPMENT

## General Tools and Equipment

- First aid kit
- Good-quality standard flashlight
- Drinking water and nourishing snack foods
- Heavy-duty pack to carry specimens
- Insect repellent
- Glow sticks for marking your path away from and back to your starting spot or vehicle

## Clothing Recommendations

- Durable rain gear for the rainy or misty shores of Lake Superior
- Warm clothing for the cool lake breezes in summer
- Water shoes or boots if you'll be hunting at the water's edge

## Specialty Tools and Equipment

- **UV-protection safety glasses:** It's a good idea to wear UV-protective glasses or goggles if you'll be doing extensive hunting ($20).

- **UV flashlights:** Convoy S2 6 watt with two rechargeable batteries (filtered, $70); Escolite 51 LED uses three AA batteries (unfiltered, $13)

Filtered UV flashlights tend to make fluorescent material stand out more from the surrounding items, but they're much more expensive than unfiltered. We feel that unfiltered flashlights produce nearly comparable results in darkness and partial-light conditions.

# REFERENCES AND RESOURCES

## Facebook Groups

- Great Lakes Rocks and Minerals
  www.facebook.com/groups/106675549490547
- Michigan Rocks and Minerals
  www.facebook.com/MichiganRocksandMinerals

## Rock Clubs

- Copper Country Rock and Mineral Club
  ccrmc.info
- Ishpeming Rock and Mineral Club
  www.ishpemingrocks.org

# THOMSONITE

Although Lake Superior agates may be more well-known, Minnesota thomsonite is the most rare, valuable, and arguably beautiful of all the gems found on the shores of Lake Superior. Minnesota thomsonite is found almost exclusively on the north shore of Lake Superior, but also much less commonly on the south shore of Lake Superior near the Keweenaw Peninsula. This particular thomsonite is world-renowned for its range of vibrant and rich colors and patterns. While other thomsonite varieties from locales across the country and world are still beautiful, they are plain in comparison—more homogenous in colors, features, and patterns. Therefore, we'll use the term "Minnesota thomsonite" to distinguish it from its less distinctive "cousins."

Thomsonite is in a class of minerals known as zeolites, which generally appear fibrous with a radiating structure. Minnesota thomsonite nodules formed within a relatively tiny subsection of the volcanic basalt along the north rim of the Lake Superior basin. As with agates, the nodules formed within small air pockets in the basalt. A solution of silica, aluminum, calcium, and other minerals seeped into the pockets and hardened. The solution also contained impurities, such as iron and copper, that gave thomsonite its range of colors. Thomsonite is comparatively softer and more brittle than Lake Superior agates, so pieces previously weathered out of the basalt were generally crushed by glacial activities. Because of this, they are rarely found in glacial till any distance from Lake Superior

Thomsonite features brilliant colors and starburst and eye-shaped patterns of dazzlingly fine "needles," making it highly sought-after for fine jewelry-making. Even pieces the size of a pea are used for making earrings and necklaces. The most sought-after and rarest thomsonite pieces are those with darker red, green, and black arrays of fine needles. A well-defined nodule the size of a quarter can fetch upwards of $500 to $1,000! That's the value of half an ounce of gold, which is more than most hobby gold prospectors would call a very good day.

So why aren't more people hunting and collecting thomsonite? It's mostly

because of its rarity and extremely limited hunting range. But don't be discouraged because you really can find high-quality specimens, especially if you are willing to invest time and resources into extracting thomsonite nodules from hard rock. Like gold prospecting, these resources include specialized machines and tools, but at a lower cost than gold-related equipment. You can also find nicely weathered-out nodules right on the Lake Superior shore, but productive hunting and collecting areas are small and heavily hunted, and some shorelines are highly restrictive or completely off-limits. We will help you navigate all of these challenges and recommend the best and most productive ways to score great (and valuable) thomsonite specimens.

## THOMSONITE FEATURES AND CHARACTERISTICS

**Colors:** The predominant colors of gem-grade thomsonite are white, pink, green, red-orange, and black. The most-prized specimens are those with dark-green or black needle arrays and with deep-red or orange highlights. The lustrous pink colors of fine thomsonite nodules are also highly sought-after by jewelry makers.

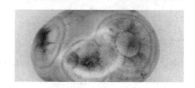

**Patterns:** The key distinguishing features of thomsonite are the eyes and the fine-needle formations. The most-prized specimens will have both, and they will be intermixed, having multiple eyes with concentric rings, inside of which there might be needle fans or arrays, possibly with additional needle arrays that are "woven" around the eye formations.

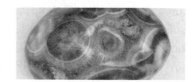

**Shape:** Most thomsonite nodules are generally round, since they formed within gas pockets in basalt. Some pieces are more elongated or oval in shape, but they are never flat or angular.

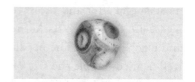

**Size:** Thomsonite nodules can be smaller than 1 millimeter in diameter, and they can be as large as 5 centimeters or more, although those are quite rare. We will generally be looking for nodules that are 1 to 2 centimeters in diameter.

# IMPOSTERS

There are a variety of rocks and minerals that will get your attention and potentially fool you. Below are those that are found most commonly in the same hunting range as thomsonite.

**Zeolites:** Other zeolites can be found in Minnesota and Michigan, especially near the Lake Superior shore. Some of these zeolites are classified as the mineral thomsonite but lack the distinctive colors and patterns that make them gem-grade. The first example is not thomsonite. The second likely is, though not in the nodular form.

**Laumontite:** Laumontite is another common imposter of thomsonite. It's found as inclusions in basalt in the form of crystal fans and arrays that are reminiscent of thomsonite, and the colors of the nodules are generally pinkish. However, close examination under a 5–10x magnifier will show clear differentiation of the crystals, and you won't find the typical thomsonite pattern and color variations.

**Paradise Beach agate:** Paradise Beach agate (a somewhat rare type of Lake Superior agate) may also fool you while hunting for thomsonite. The good news is that these beautiful gems are highly sought-after in their own right! Paradise Beach agates share many characteristics with thomsonite, including small size, rounded nodules, eye formations, vibrant pink, red, and green colors, and sometimes even fine details that look a bit like needle fans. However, close examinations under a 5–10x magnifier will show that these aren't needles. Paradise Beach agates feel "harder" than thomsonite, and they might have pitting, peeling, or visible banding, which are all uncommon in thomsonite.

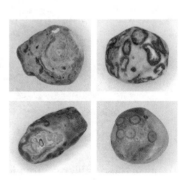

**Mesolite:** Mesolite is another potential imposter of thomsonite because of its fine needle sprays, which are sometimes radial, and because it's often found in white-and-pink color combinations. But mesolite doesn't have well-defined eyes, and its colors are dissimilar to the vibrant pinks and greens in thomsonite.

# THOMSONITE PROSPECTING REGION

The productive hunting range for thomsonite is extremely small, as shown on the map below. While specimens can be found within about a 30-mile radius from the oval, they are more by chance and good fortune. The epicenter of thomsonite hunting is the point of Good Harbor Bay, as shown.

**Thomsonite Prospecting Region**

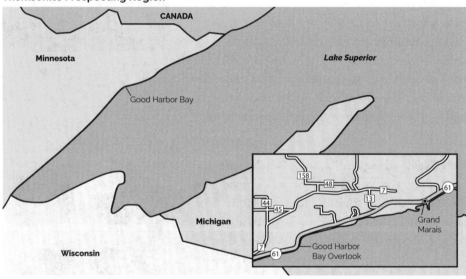

Because the productive area for finding thomsonite is so small, once you've made the drive to the area, thankfully there's little driving left to do. However, time is well spent driving around a little to check out sand and gravel deposits (such as in gravel pits), road cuts, and other areas with exposed bedrock and broken chunks on the ground, and shoreline areas with broken chunks of bedrock or lake-tumbled stones.

## Safety Factors

Before diving into the prospecting and hunting details, let's talk about safety. These are the most important considerations when prospecting for thomsonite.

- **Walking or working near the roadway:** In many cases it's against the law to work in close proximity to roadways, especially major roadways, like Highway 61 that runs along the north shore of Lake Superior. People have been fined or arrested. If you find a less-traveled roadway with exposed bedrock faces to hunt, you need to take precautions for both yourself and motorists. Keep a safe distance from the road, and don't let your actions cause rock to tumble onto the roadway.

- **Hunting in high wind and surf:** Windy or stormy weather brings rough surf that deposits new material on the shoreline, but it also brings danger. Listen to your instincts; keep a safe distance or simply wait for the storm to subside before venturing out.

- **Rock breaking, at the collection site and in your workshop:** Safety glasses are required anytime you'll be breaking rock. Prescription glasses aren't enough; you'll still need safety goggles worn over them. You might even need a face shield if working more aggressively, or a helmet if there is a chance of falling rock—although it might just be best to find a less dangerous hunting venue.

- **Working with drilling and grinding equipment:** When working with power tools, always follow the manufacturer's safety instructions. And since thomsonite is such a delicate gemstone, there is all the more reason to be patient and cautious when extracting nodules from host rock.

## LAKE SUPERIOR SHORELINE

Just to the north and east of Good Harbor is a publicly accessible shorefront and wayside rest at the mouth of Cutface Creek. There are other accessible areas nearby, as well, that may be worth doing some prospecting in, but they might not be as easy to access or could be on privately owned property. If you find a viable hunting spot, you'll need to determine land ownership and ask the owners for permission. We provide some helpful suggestions in this regard in the Lake Superior Agates chapter (see page 28). You can also check with the Thomsonite Beach Inn & Suites as to whether they would allow you to hunt and collect along their section of the shoreline; if you are really serious about the experience, you might want to book a week at their resort.

Lake-tumbled stones along the shore

For shoreline areas with stones that have been nicely tumbled by waves and sand, the best bet is to sit where you can find a concentration of tumbled stones that range from smaller than a pea to the size of a quarter. As with hunting all gems and minerals, patience and persistence will serve you well, because the pieces you're looking for are so small, and there are many other brightly colored stones that will catch your eye. Start by examining stones in the top layer, and then gently brush away successive layers after inspecting each one to see if there are any thomsonite "prospects." This is a studious but very calming activity, since you'll be listening to the rhythm of the waves all the while. Have a 5–10x magnifier along to inspect for the fine details of thomsonite patterns.

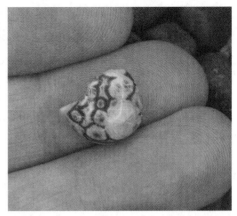

Light pink and white with a deep-green band give this little treasure away. On the flip side are several striking eye formations with needle fans.

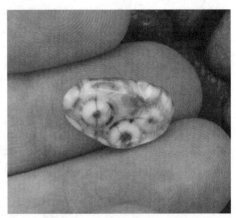

The bright pink and white colors on this nice-size piece practically glow, even without a polish.

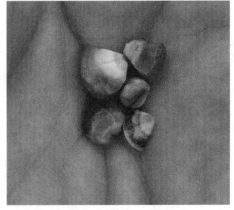

This handful of tiny beauties shows why you need to think and look small, very small. The pieces with the deep green and salmon pink are a little easier to spot. Sometimes you just need to pick up handfuls of rocks and sift through them.

# EXPOSED BEDROCK AND BOULDERS

When not hunting on the lakeshore, you will be examining bedrock walls or already weathered-out boulders and chunks of basalt lying on the ground, with the latter being the easiest to work with of the two. You will need a large and sturdy collecting bucket, pack, or pouch, and you'll want to be close to your vehicle, due to the weight of the rocks. Sometimes a small wagon or ATV may be called for to cart your rock pieces and chunks back to your vehicle.

You'll be inspecting bedrock walls and loose chunks to see if they have any pink, green, or white inclusions that might be embedded thomsonite nodules. Always start with the chunks that have broken free because that means you don't have to do any chisel, sledgehammer, or pickaxe work. You may be surprised by how many chunks of bedrock with exposed thomsonite nodules have been left behind or are newly weathered-out (especially in the spring). While larger thomsonite nodules with well-defined features can be identified by the naked eye, a 5–10x magnifier will help you inspect for the ultrafine-needle fans that are characteristic of thomsonite, helping you differentiate it from imposters like laumontite, agates, and other types of zeolites.

While in prospecting mode, even finding the tiniest nodules of 1 to 3 millimeters in diameter in a piece of basalt lets you know you're on the right track. It's exactly like doing "test pans" when gold prospecting to see if you are getting any gold flecks. When you find a loose chunk with probable nodules, stow it in your collecting bucket or pouch; you'll need better tools and lighting and a good work surface to remove the nodules intact. There might be an even larger nodule inside, and you could easily damage or destroy a nodule worth hundreds of dollars by using rough tools like chisels and hammers. For nodules embedded in a rock wall, you need to inspect the surface 3 to 5 inches away from the visible nodule(s) for seams, and then use chisels, sledgehammers, and pickaxes to dislodge chunks containing the nodules; the Keokuk Geodes chapter provides a good process outline for breaking up hard rock with sledges and pickaxes (see page 153). Make sure you are wearing safety goggles, and use only the amount of force necessary to break chunks free, to limit any potential damage to embedded thomsonite nodules.

Here, you see a lot of loose, broken up bedrock. Do not assume that all of the pieces that contain desirable nodules have already been taken.

Less broken rock is lying around here, perhaps requiring more work with pickaxes, chisels, and sledgehammers.

This nice chunk has good-size nodules at the surface that can be extracted in the workshop at home.

Some days, good luck will shine on you, and you might find a nice piece of thomsonite already broken free!

## OTHER HUNTING VENUES

There are undoubtedly thomsonite specimens to be found in nearby gravel pits and streambeds, but your productivity level will be substantially lower. The hunting methods and means for gaining approval to hunt in these venues are similar to that of Lake Superior agates along the north shore of Lake Superior (see page 23). One notable difference is that you'll be looking for much smaller specimens, so you'll need to be crouching or even crawling along on the sand and gravel. The other difference is that you'll be looking for thomsonite nodules embedded in host basalt stone, akin to finding Lake Superior agate nodules still in their host rock.

## EXTRACTING THOMSONITE NODULES FROM BEDROCK

Working thomsonite nodules out of bedrock is comparable in many respects to gold prospecting. You start by finding small or even miniscule amounts of the desired material mixed in with or embedded within much larger amounts of surrounding or host material. In gold prospecting, the material is called "pay dirt." With thomsonite there isn't a comparable term, but you might call large chunks of rock that show thomsonite nodules "pay rock." And as with gold prospecting, you'll need to collect a substantial amount of the "pay" material that will be "concentrated" or worked down to yield gemstones.

Once you've returned home with your buckets of bedrock chunks, you can inspect them and start working free any nodules visible at the surface level. Small nodules that are partially embedded can usually be broken free with a hammer and chisel, but extracting nodules that are higher grade or more completely embedded in the host basalt may call for rotary tool carving or core drilling. These processes are shown later in this chapter.

Sometimes you'll want to split the bedrock into smaller pieces in hopes of discovering additional nodules. In that case, start by identifying any natural cracks or seams, and then use a hammer and chisel to break the rock apart. Once again, never use more force than necessary because there might be a prized nodule along one of the seams that could easily be chipped or broken. **And always remember your protective eyewear!**

## Chisel Method

Use this method for small whole nodules near seams or edges, where the thomsonite nodule will pop loose from the host rock, likely with a bit of the host rock attached. Saw or sand away any remaining host rock. Continue working the

There's a small nodule near the edge of this bedrock chunk, and there's a visible seam, as well, so it's a great candidate for the chisel method.

Place the head of the chisel into the fissure, and tap firmly to break up the host rock.

A thomsonite nodule with host rock still attached

bedrock chunk until you've removed all of the nodules that are near the edge or close to fissures and seams.

The final step in removing the last of the bedrock is a medium-grit tumble in a vibratory tumbler for 2 to 4 hours. For more information on tumbling, and grinding and polishing, including recommended equipment and supplies, see my comprehensive beginner's guide to the art of lapidary, *Gemstone Tumbling, Cutting, Drilling & Cabochon Making: A Simple Guide to Finishing Rough Stones*. In addition to that guide, here are a few special considerations for working with thomsonite.

- Don't tumble thomsonite with harder rocks, like agates. We recommend a mix of basalt and ceramic tumbling media. After tumbling, remove the stones carefully, and check to ensure that all bedrock is off. You can also use a 180 grit grinding wheel or disk to get the last bits of bedrock off. After that, you can proceed through the fine-grit tumbling and polishing stages in the vibratory tumbler.

- For pieces that will be set in silver or gold, instead of tumbling, you can polish only the top face. Grind the backside flat on your lapidary grinder, and coat it with epoxy to strengthen and "stabilize" the stone. You can then dome polish the top surface. Your thomsonite piece is now ready to be wire wrapped or set in silver or another metal of your choice.

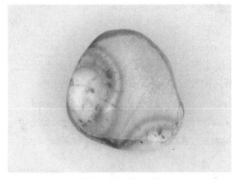 

Dome-polished thomsonite pieces

Here are two partially exposed whole nodules that will likely break free intact after "carving" around the perimeter of the nodule with the Rotary Tool Method (see next page).

## Rotary Tool Method

For smaller pieces that are partially exposed, use a rotary tool to carve a groove in the host rock around the nodule until it pops free or can be gently pulled from the host rock. A rotary tool causes vibration, so don't use it for more-valuable pieces. Next, a vibratory tumbler is used to remove the last of the bedrock and to polish the specimen, as detailed on page 70. **Safety note: Cutting and grinding rocks releases rock dust, which is a health hazard. Always wear a respirator, and work in well-ventilated conditions.**

A small thomsonite nodule with a groove cut around it

Nodules extracted with the rotary tool method

## Core Drill Method

This method is the best way to extract deeply embedded thomsonite nodules from bedrock. It's also the safest way to extract large and high-grade thomsonite nodules, which can be worth hundreds or even thousands of dollars, without shattering them. A core of the host rock is removed, with the nodule still inside, and then lapidary tools are used to free the nodule from the core.

For ultra-high-grade nodules, we strongly recommend that you cover the exposed portion with 5-minute epoxy. Goop the epoxy on liberally, and then **let it set for a full 24 hours.**

Use a standard drill with a 2"-diameter diamond-coated coring bit, and supply a steady stream of water where you are drilling to keep the cutting face of the bit cool.

If the nodule is close to a corner of the bedrock piece, you may be able to drill from the top and then from the side to fully cut the core loose (see first photo below). This is preferred, if possible, because with this method the core doesn't need to be chiseled free.

If the nodule is too far from the edge, you will only be able to drill around the nodule from one direction. Drill down far enough to make sure you have cut deeper than the nodule (see second photo). Then insert a small flat chisel down to the bottom of the drilled rim on the side farthest from the nodule, and tap with the hammer to break the core free.

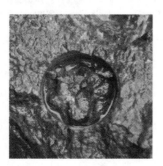

If there is a lot of host rock still around the nodule, you can use a lapidary saw to surgically cut away larger chunks of material. After that, you can use a flat lapidary grinding machine to remove almost all of the remaining host rock. A 180-mesh disk will work best to gradually grind away material until you're close to the edges of the nodule. These nodules will then go into the vibratory tumbler to remove the last of the host rock and to polish the specimen, as detailed on page 70. See the Lapidary Arts chapter for details on sawing and grinding.

The core drill method was used to free this museum-grade piece that was shaped and buffed to show multiple thomsonite and other zeolite occurrences in a single chamber.

# TOOLS AND EQUIPMENT

## General Tools and Equipment

- Safety goggles
- Durable work gloves
- 5-gallon buckets
- Handheld drill for core drilling

## Specialty Tools and Equipment

- **Rotary tool and diamond cutting bits:** Dremel complete kit with tool and a large set of cutting, grinding, sanding, and polishing heads ($100)
- **Diamond-coated 25mm coring bit:** Diamond coring bits have crushed diamond coating around the bottom rim of the bit ($12).
- **Sledgehammer, pickaxe, chisels:** Refer to Keokuk Geodes chapter.

# REFERENCES AND RESOURCES

## Books

- Lynch, Bob, and Dan Lynch. *Lake Superior Rocks & Minerals: A Field Guide to the Lake Superior Area.* Adventure Publications, 2008.

## Magazines and Periodicals

- *Rock & Gem Magazine*

## Rock Shops

- Beaver Bay Agate Shop & Jewelry, Beaver Bay, MN
  www.beaverbayagateshop.com

## Rock Clubs

- Carlton County Gem & Mineral Club, Cloquet, MN
  www.facebook.com/groups/891164997610511

# COPPER

At current market prices, gold is valued at nearly $2,000 per ounce, silver at $20 per ounce, and copper at less than $1 per ounce. So why would anyone spend their time prospecting for copper? This is a question I asked myself many times before I began to get acquainted with the treasures that can be found in the Upper Peninsula of Michigan, or "UP" for short. As it turns out, there are truly magnificent copper specimens to be found, and they can also be quite valuable. Some of the value is in the sheer size of "native copper" masses, including pieces that weigh from several hundred pounds to hundreds of tons. "Native" is a geology term that refers to a mass of a pure or almost pure element, not combined with other minerals.

The largest native copper mass ever discovered was 527 tons! It was found inside the Minesota Mine ("Minnesota" was misspelled with one "n" when the company was incorporated). The largest "float copper" specimen ever found is 28 tons. The geology term "float" refers to any material that's been moved by erosion (ice age glaciers in this case). Float copper is found as smooth, solid masses of any size. These copper masses are also sometimes known as "drift copper," with "drift" referring to material moved specifically by glaciers.

In addition to large specimens, there are many other factors that add to the value and allure of copper prospecting. Perhaps foremost is the astounding beauty and diversity of the crystalline forms and structures that occur in UP copper. Even

after a lifetime of hunting, an avid copper prospector can continue to discover new and unique forms never before seen. Also to be found are copper specimens with silver crystals within, and float pieces known as "half-breeds" that are a mixture of native copper and native silver. Pure float silver and pure silver crystals are sometimes found, although these pure forms are exceedingly rare. Calcite crystals can be found with fine copper particulates inside of them, creating a stunningly beautiful rose coloration. These are quite rare and are highly prized specimens.

As if that weren't enough to excite you about copper prospecting on the Upper Peninsula, there is an absolute abundance of other beautiful and valuable gems and minerals, many of which are greatly enhanced by copper mineralization or copper "replacement." Two of the most prominent of these gemstones are covered later in this book: greenstone (also known as chlorastrolite) and datolite. Both of these are highly sought-after for display and jewelry-making. In addition, there is a rare and valuable Lake Superior agate type known as the copper replacement agate.

Finally, there is the lapidary aspect of copper prospecting. Turning your finds into gorgeous display or jewelry pieces adds a significant level of enjoyment and reward. For large pieces of float copper or distinctive crystal formations, your goal will be to highlight and accentuate the natural beauty of your specimens. With smaller or less distinctive finds, you might decide to use them for jewelry-making, as individual pieces, or possibly even melting them down for metalwork.

Happily, there are publicly accessible sites available for copper prospecting. Most of these sites are located on the premises of defunct copper mines and frequently involve working through tailings, or waste piles, from these mines. The Keweenaw Peninsula Chamber of Commerce in Houghton, Michigan, will even provide you with maps and directions to the mine sites. This is subject to change, of course, but this should be your first stop when you are just beginning. Additionally, the Copper Country and Ishpeming rock and mineral clubs both have annual shows that provide up-to-date information about which mines allow public hunting—both during their shows and for independent prospecting activities. In Houghton, Michigan, the A. E. Seaman Mineral Museum provides a world-class exhibit and geological research experience that beginners and long-time copper prospectors will enjoy.

# IMPOSTERS

You will find many greenish rocks that have no or very little copper. All of these imposters can be quickly ruled out with a metal detector; if the metal detector doesn't indicate the presence of metal, it's not copper. The surface of copper oxidizes to a greenish or bluish color, but a "scratch test" can reveal whether there's a bright-orange copper color beneath the weathered surface. But since copper is often well beneath the surface of its host rock (basalt, quartz, or calcite), it's usually not possible to just scratch away the surface layer to expose the copper, so the metal detector is the only reliable test.

**Chlorite:** This is generally found in a nodular form with a very deep-green coloration, but it can also be an overlay on a large section of basalt.

**Epidote:** Epidote is found as bright lime-green overlays on basalt, and also as nodular inclusions with brilliant green crystals and sometimes even copper crystals!

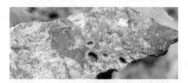

**Chrysocolla:** This is most often found as turquoise overlays on more-reddish-colored basalt specimens. It can be collectible when found as larger mineral inclusions.

**Greenstone:** Greenstone (also known as chlorastrolite) is the highly sought-after Michigan state gemstone. Like chlorite, it features a very deep-green husk and is nodular in form. Inside, there is often a bright-white calcite center, and there are usually finely detailed needle arrays.

# COPPER TYPES

Copper can be found in many forms, shapes, and settings. The following photos show some of the most common. See page 99 for suggested books that provide detailed information and descriptions. And remember that while you can sometimes find copper just by visual identification, 90% of the time you'll be finding it with a metal detector because it's embedded in host rock or buried in the earth.

**Float:** Float copper is a mass of copper that is typically smooth due to glacial movement. Pieces up to a few pounds are common. Large masses, such as the 200-pound piece in the second photo, are quite rare.

**Thin layer or flake:** This copper is less than 1 mm in thickness and generally not worthy of collecting or showing, making it something of a nuisance find.

**Small crystals in matrix:** These tiny concentrations of copper in host stone are not of much value, but the crystals can be beautiful under magnification.

**Copper "blobs":** Unlike small crystals, these small "blobs" aren't even of much interest under magnification.

**Shot copper:** These are small copper pieces spread across a piece of host rock. With a little work, this can yield a pretty display with a "constellation" of shiny copper. First photo is as found; second photo is after a 48-hour vinegar soak and scrub.

**Fine copper particles in matrix:** These ultra-fine particles will trigger your metal detector, but you'll learn to tune your detector and ignore the faint signals this common type renders.

**Seam with quartz or calcite:** This common type has a vein of copper running through white quartz or calcite. Larger crystals are often found in these seams and should be handled carefully until you can use a chemical treatment to remove them intact (see the Lapidary Arts chapter).

**Copper in epidote cavity:** These copper crystals formed inside a pocket of vibrant lime-green epidote. Under magnification, this common type can make beautiful specimen pieces.

**Copper replacement agate:** Calcite crystals in these agates dissolved and were later replaced by copper. These are very rare and beautiful, and larger banded specimens can be very valuable.

**Fern copper:** This rare type of copper crystal resembles a fern. These are very rare and quite valuable, especially larger specimens.

**Native American copper artifacts:** Native American copper artifacts, such as arrow and spear points, are very rare but can be found in Michigan and Wisconsin.

**Complex and compound crystal structures:** This museum-grade specimen shows the most highly sought-after, beautiful, and valuable copper specimen type. These are very rare, especially for specimens bigger than a dime.

**Copper specks in quartz crystals:** These tiny flecks of copper floating in quartz crystal lend a rosy glow to the crystal. These are extremely rare.

**Chisel chip:** Copper miners broke down very large copper masses with chisels and sledgehammers. These chips are generally rare but more common in some mines.

**Copper with silver/pure silver:** Some copper crystals contain segments of silver or, in rare cases, pure silver crystals. These are quite rare and highly prized as specimen pieces, especially when larger than 1/8". Some truly magnificent silver crystals have been found at copper mines.

**Copper wires:** Copper wires are thin copper filaments that "grew" inside a calcite vein within the basalt mass. These are especially valuable when longer than an inch in length.

## COPPER PROSPECTING REGIONS

The map below shows the general regions where Michigan copper can be reliably found. Our primary focus will be on the Keweenaw Peninsula (Region 1), which has the highest concentration of known deposits. It's also the source of the vast majority of copper found in Region 2. Therefore, Region 1 is likely to be the only place that you'll find intact and crisply defined crystalline copper specimens; most copper found more than 20 miles from its source is float copper that has been broken and weathered by glaciation.

Copper found in Region 2 is almost exclusively float copper that was transported by glacial movements. As far as hunting for float copper versus hunting for copper in crystalline form, neither is "better." It all comes down to personal preference.

**Copper Prospecting Regions**

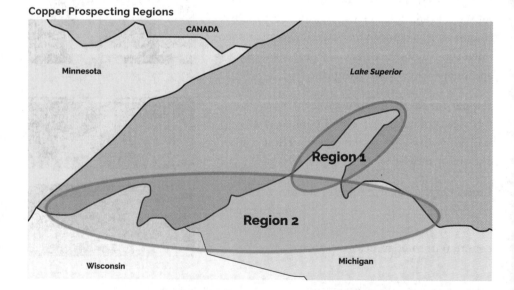

**Region 1:** Michigan's Keweenaw Peninsula is a literal treasure trove for rock-hounds. There are good hunting locations all along the 70-mile-long peninsula. All manner of copper specimens can be found in tailing piles at abandoned copper mining sites. Float copper can be found as pieces the size of a dime up to several hundred pounds. In addition, there are many other gems to be found, such as greenstone (chlorastrolite) and datolite.

**Region 2:** There is a good chance of finding copper along the entire Upper Peninsula of Michigan and the far northern rim of Wisconsin. The majority of specimens will be float copper, and they will be found primarily in woodlands, fields, and along rivers. There were some copper mining operations in this area, though none nearly as large as the mines on the Keweenaw Peninsula. And most of Wisconsin's copper mine sites are now covered with dense vegetation, making them difficult to locate and navigate.

# GENERAL PROSPECTING AND HUNTING PROCESS

Whether hunting on tailing piles or for float copper in forests and fields, modern copper prospecting is done almost exclusively with metal detectors. Copper can be spotted by its bright-green oxidization or its crystalline structures, but this is unlikely unless you happen across some freshly exposed material that has also been washed by rain. So before proceeding further in this chapter, it would be helpful to acquaint yourself with the Metal Detecting chapter in this book (page 244). It describes how to select makes and models that are well suited to hunting for metal ores, like gold and copper, and gives general usage guidelines. For copper hunting (as with gold hunting), it's extremely helpful to have both a regular metal detector and a "pinpointer" to more efficiently sort through material as you dig down towards the specimens.

If you're keenly interested in finding crystal specimens, your best bet will be to hunt on old mine dump piles, or at least on the grounds of the old mines. The Keweenaw Peninsula Chamber of Commerce can recommend publicly accessible sites, saving you from having to acquire access permissions. Hunting on old mine dump piles requires significant stamina, coordination, and even some upper body strength for moving large stones. You'll be climbing on large piles of jagged rock chunks and carefully moving and tossing things aside or down the pile, either to allow your metal detector to send signals deeper into the pile or in response to a signal. You'll also be kneeling on hard and rocky ground while pounding on rocks to break them and expose the copper inside. Sometimes you'll be fortunate enough to show up at an old mine site to find piles that have had old material stripped away or sections of piles that have been bulldozed flat specifically for hobby prospecting. This latter opportunity happens at least annually at sites that the local rock club uses for paid hunting trips.

For float copper hunting, it is a bit more difficult to gain permission to hunt, on both private and public land, and it's much more of a hit-or-miss process to find productive locales. Similar to hunting for other gemstones, you should start by locating the source (mining sites, in this case) and then drawing concentric rings outward; the closer you are to the source the better your chances of locating good-size specimens. Once you find a spot and obtain permission, the level of required physical strength and stamina is somewhat less than that required to work mine dump piles, but there will still be sometimes-rugged hiking, digging for items, and hauling your finds to your vehicle. GPS can come in handy if you locate a monster specimen that weighs over 100 pounds; you might need to mark its location and return later to retrieve it. GPS is also useful for noting locations where you've found float copper–developing a "heat map" of places where you've had success.

## Safety Factors

When you're working with tools like picks and hammers, it's important to maintain a safe distance of at least 8 feet between yourself and other hunters. One swing of a pick or sledgehammer could result in traumatic injuries, either from flying rock chunks or being struck by the tool itself.

- **Safety glasses:** It's essential that you use high-quality safety glasses or goggles when working with picks and hammers. You might even consider wearing a full-face shield to protect more than just your eyes.

- **Earplugs:** Believe it or not, working around a lot of people doing pick and hammer work on hard rock can get quite loud. A simple pair of earplugs will help you avoid a pounding headache after a long day of hunting and extraction.

- **Pay attention:** When you are working on mine tailing piles with large and jagged rocks, it's important to move slowly. With each step, take your time in planting your feet to ensure that the rocks are stable enough to hold your full weight. As you begin to dig into the pile to hone in on signals from your metal detector, look first before carefully tossing unwanted rocks away, and toss them safely away from any other hunters in your vicinity. When you or other people working on the same pile move larger rocks, the pile can become unstable, causing landslides of large and jagged rocks, so always work at a measured pace, and be alert to the people working above and below you.

- **Take breaks:** Working on mine tailing piles is physically strenuous, so take regular breaks and stay hydrated. On hot summer days, move to a shady area periodically and take a sustained break. Remember that whatever you collect needs to be carried back to your vehicle, so save some energy for your return trip.

- **Wildlife:** When you are hunting in remote areas, and forests in particular, be alert to your surroundings for large or aggressive animals, such as bears, wolves, moose, mountain lions, and, of course, people. We strongly recommend hunting in small groups or at least pairs, and it's important to let people know your planned hunting route and expected return time before going out.

- **Weather:** Weather can change quickly. Plan ahead by getting a current forecast, and then regularly monitor conditions throughout the day. You might want to keep a hooded rain poncho with you, considering the frequency of rain and mist coming off of Lake Superior.

# MINE DUMPS

There are literally hundreds of abandoned mines in the Upper Peninsula of Michigan, but not all of them are open to hobby prospecting, and many of them have been hunted extensively without any regular turnover of the tailing piles. Some mines are open for public copper hunting, and most of these don't charge a fee. The map and table that follow show some of the more popular sites, but you must check into the mine's current policy before going in. Consider joining one of the rock clubs, even if you can't attend regularly, so that you can gain the access provided to members and get information about good hunting times and locations.

**Popular Mines for Copper Prospecting**

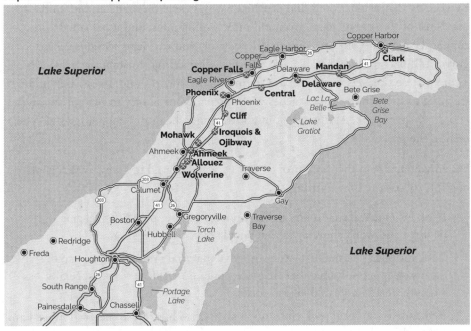

**Popular Mines for Copper Prospecting**

| Mine Name | Copper | Greenstone (Chlorastrolite) | Datolite | Silver | Copper Agates |
|---|---|---|---|---|---|
| Ahmeek | Yes | | | | |
| Allouez | Yes | | | Yes | |
| Central | Yes | Yes | Yes | Yes | |
| Clark | Yes | Yes | Yes | Yes | |
| Cliff | Yes | Yes | | Yes | |
| Copper Falls | Yes | | Yes | | |
| Delaware | Yes | Yes | Yes | Yes | |
| Iroquois | Yes | | Yes | | |
| Mandan | Yes | Yes | | Yes | |
| Mohawk | Yes | | | | |
| Ojibway | Yes | | | | |
| Phoenix | Yes | Yes | | Yes | |
| Wolverine | Yes | | | Yes | Yes |

## Hunting on Mine Tailing Piles

If you are just getting started, before going to the mine, there's a wonderful exercise you can do that will accelerate your rate of success. Throughout the Keweenaw Peninsula, you'll find crushed basalt gravel on roads and in landscaping. Most of this gravel came from old mine tailing piles, and it is loaded with copper. Using just your pinpoint metal detector, you can scan sections of this gravel and become comfortable and familiar with sifting through the gravel to locate a piece that has copper in it. Getting a little success under your belt and learning to spot small copper pieces will sharpen your ability to recognize rough and dirty specimens. And you just might turn up a beautiful copper crystal specimen in the process!

When you arrive at the mine property, do a walk-around to assess which spots might be best suited for hunting.

- Look for material that might be freshly moved or exposed. It will generally be dirty and won't show signs that people have been digging in it.

- Look for piles that make it easier to move material around, which usually means steep piles. Remember that steep piles pose safety risks, especially when there are large and jagged rocks.

- Remember that local rock clubs often arrange to have fresh material moved and exposed for club-sponsored hunts. These are great opportunities for beginning copper prospectors!

This is a copper hunter's dream, a big pile of dirty and freshly moved mine tailings!

This rock is clean, which means that it hasn't been turned over recently. Also, the pile isn't very steep, so it will be a lot of work to move things around and expose new material.

This shows a flat area of clean rock. Unless you have an ultra-high-end detector that can do advanced discrimination or deep readings, you're unlikely to have much success.

Here is clean rock, but the pile is steep, so you can move rocks around (carefully) to expose new material.

Once you've found a spot that you want to hunt, it's time to tune your metal detector (see page 251). Here are reminders of a few key points.

- Perform ground balance to reduce "chatter."
- Choose the coins or precious metals setting.
- Set the discrimination level based on the likely amount of junk present at the site (such as iron and aluminum); we choose a moderate setting if we feel there won't be a lot of junk.

Once you begin detecting, make sure that you keep the detector head moving in broad, deliberate, and slow sweeping motions over your target area. Wait until you get a sustained and high-signal-strength reading of at least 80 (the example at right shows 93). There is so much fine copper present that lower readings will have you "chasing" very tiny specimens or specimens with very fine copper embedded throughout.

Stop the detector head over the spot with the strongest signal strength, and make a visual note of where the center point of the detector head is located. Your detector might also show a depth reading, such as the example above, which shows a depth of 8 inches.

Use your hands to move away larger pieces of rock and debris, placing it all in one place; this allows you to rescan it to see if the copper is still in the hole or in the material you moved away.

Use the pinpoint detector to narrow the focus of the search and then to verify that the specimen you believe holds copper gives a strong signal.

Here are examples of rough and dirty copper that is visible on the surface. The pinpointer will ring loudest when it's next to the features shown in the photos.

Note the small point sticking up.

A thin vein of reddish copper running along the white calcite seam

Note the rounded "blob" on the top right.

A thin vein of copper along the top edge— probably a small plate or sheet of copper that can be removed intact with a chisel and hammer

A large crystalline copper structure, encased in basalt, that can be exposed with some gentle hammering

Note the use of the pinpoint button on this detector (top right photo) that provides more-detailed readings and the precise location of the item generating the strongest signal. This is especially helpful for specimens at greater depth.

# Exposing Copper from Basalt Chunks at Old Mine Sites

Much of the copper to be found on copper mine tailing piles is still inside host rock and not visible. Sometimes these chunks are quite large, so you'll want to break them down before putting them in your pack.

- Work on a hard, flat surface.
- Look for existing cracks or fractures in the host stone, and break away stone on the side of the fracture that offers the least damage to a visible specimen.
- Strike the host rock with the least amount of force needed to break it up.
- Once you have broken off most of the host rock, you might decide to finish the job at home if you are concerned about damaging the specimen.

Specimen 1: Agate nodule with a trace amount of copper that's not visible to the naked eye

Specimen 2: A small copper "blob"

Specimen 3: A nice row of small copper crystals in a calcite seam; note the shatter resistant safety glasses!

Specimen 4: Some shimmering green epidote nodules, with copper and calcite crystals inside

# FIELDS AND FORESTS, BEACHES, AND GRAVEL PITS

Finding productive hunting locales for float copper is as much art as it is science. The distribution of float copper by glacial activity is so random that it boils down to sample hunting and recording of results. As with hunting for gold nuggets, you will run across occasional patches that yield many larger and high-quality specimens. These patches might be as large as a football field, or even significantly larger. Meticulously documenting your hunting activities is critical because it might take you several outings to start getting good "hits." Joining a rock club or Facebook group can be helpful in learning general information about successful locales. If you live out of town and only visit occasionally, it's worth asking whether anyone will take you on a guided hunt for a modest fee. One final tip is to remember that large things very often follow small things; don't get frustrated after finding a few dime-size specimens, but do start bypassing weaker signals, as larger copper masses will set off loud, strong signals.

Some beaches that have been hunted successfully include Eagle River, Esrey Park, Gratiot River, and Pete's. Make sure to check with the local chamber of commerce for information. And remember that you need permission to hunt on private land; we provide some helpful suggestions on this throughout the Lake Superior Agates chapter.

## Field and Forest Hunting Scenario

When hunting in a field or forest, you'll be covering much larger expanses of ground than at mine sites (where your detector will pick up signals quite regularly), so take a little time to think about how you want to cover the territory you'll be hunting in. Other than that, your process will be similar to hunting at mine sites.

- Cover ground with wide, sweeping motions.

- After identifying a strong and persistent signal, use your detector's pinpointing feature to determine the depth of the object and exactly where to dig.

- Begin digging, depositing the removed material in one place—it might still include the copper specimen if it was at a shallower depth than indicated by the detector.

- Use the pinpoint handheld detector to isolate the specimen, scooping out and sifting handfuls of dirt and rocks.

We found a terrific 5-ounce float copper specimen that will polish up and display nicely!

## Beach Hunting Scenario

As with hunting in fields and forests, you'll be methodically working across large expanses of ground with wide, sweeping motions of the metal detector. You won't have to do any digging, and your specimens will be nicely washed and tumbled, making them relatively easy to pick out by their greenish blue tints or their soft, glowing copper color. The downside of lakeshore hunting is that the easily accessible rocky beaches get hunted heavily, so it's important to hunt them immediately after big storms or soon after winter snow and ice melt.

# TOOLS AND EQUIPMENT

## General Tools and Equipment

- First aid kit
- 5-gallon buckets
- Shovel if float copper hunting
- Hand trowel
- 5–10x magnifier and/or a 30–60x loupe
- Heavy-duty pack to carry specimens
- Spray bottle and a small nylon or wire brush to clean things off for inspection
- Dinking water and nourishing snack foods
- Insect repellent
- Sunscreen
- Packing material such as newspaper or packing paper to wrap any delicate specimens

## Clothing Recommendations

- Durable rain gear, since the UP can be rainy and misty
- Supportive and durable hiking and climbing boots (steel-toed boots aren't recommended because they can conflict with your metal detector)
- Safety glasses or a face shield, since you (and others nearby) might need to break large rocks
- Hat with eye shade
- Non-shaded glasses if you wear eyeglasses, because sunglasses reduce your ability to spot subtle color differences
- Heavy-duty work gloves
- Full-length jeans or other work pants

## Specialty Tools and Equipment

- **Reliable cell phone and service:** This is a must, especially in remote areas and when working on steep tailing piles.
- **GPS apps for your phone:** Use these to note hunting spots where you've had success hunting float copper (many are free).
- **Metal detectors:** Refer to the Metal Detecting chapter for recommended makes, models, and costs ($300–700).

- **Pinpoint metal detector:** Refer to the Metal Detecting chapter for more details ($150).

- **Knee and wrist protectors:** For hunting close to the ground ($25)

- **5–10x lighted magnifier:** Carson MiniBrite is one good model ($11).

- **Lighted 30–60x jeweler's loupe:** Dreame, Jarlink, etc. ($10–15)

- **Safety glasses/goggles or face shield:** For protection while breaking rock ($25)

- **Rock hammer pick:** by Estwing ($30)

- **Chisel of medium width and thickness:** by Estwing ($25)

- **Mini sledgehammer:** by Estwing ($35)

- **Half-Inch mesh plastic classifier pan:** For sorting small specimens out of sand and dirt ($15)

# REFERENCES AND RESOURCES

## Books

- Wilson, Marc L., and Stanley J. Dyl II. *The Michigan Copper Country: The Mineralogical Record March–April 1992.* The Mineralogical Record, 1992.

- Heinrich, E.W. *Minerology of Michigan.* Updated and revised by George W. Robinson. Michigan Technical University, 2004.

- Molloy, Lawrence. *A Guide to Michigan's Historic Keweenaw Copper District.* Great Lakes Geoscience, 2008. (This is an updated version of *Copper Country Road Trips*, with photographs, maps, hidden mines and rock piles, and tours.)

## Shops with Copper Specimens and Information

- Keweenaw Gem & Gift (also known as Copper Connection), Houghton, MI
  copperconnection.com

- The Wood'n Spoon, Mohawk, MI
  www.facebook.com/TheWoodnSpoon

- Copper World, Calumet, MI
  www.calumetcopper.com

- Quincy Mine, Hancock, MI
  www.quincymine.com

- Red Metal Minerals, Ontonagon, MI
  www.redmetalminerals.com

- Caledonia Mine, Ontonagon, MI
  www.caledoniamine.com

## Facebook Groups

- Michigan Rocks & Minerals
  www.facebook.com/MichiganRocksandMinerals

## Rock and Mineral Clubs

- Copper Country Rock and Mineral Club
  ccrmc.info

- Ishpeming Rock and Mineral Club
  www.ishpemingrocks.org

## Museums and Educational Institutions

- A. E. Seaman Mineral Museum
  museum.mtu.edu

# GOLD

Because gold has been the most sought-after mineral since the dawn of civilization, it's not surprising that most concentrated large quantities of surface (or close to the surface) gold has already been recovered. In the Black Hills of South Dakota, tens of millions of ounces of gold have been extracted, either through lode mining (hard rock mining and processing to extract the gold) or prospecting for placer gold (gold that has weathered out of its host material).

There are millions of ounces of placer (pronounced "plasser") gold still to be found within massive alluvial deposits (material moved and deposited by running water) scattered around the Black Hills. The modern-day prospector who uses proven methods, tools, and equipment will be rewarded. With hard work, patience, and a bit of good fortune, prospectors can enjoy their hobby and make a decent amount of money to pay for their expenses. However, as so many experienced prospectors have told us, **even the best and most lucky know it's only a hobby!**

Despite years of prospecting, there are countless venues where gold can still be found (especially in the Black Hills), and many of them are on public lands that aren't restricted by prospecting and mining claims. Like other gems and minerals featured in this book, your prospecting effort starts with researching the areas where gold can be found. If you get to the point of wanting to stake your own claim, which is neither recommended nor necessary for beginning gold

prospectors, you'll need to research information about property ownership and recorded claims. This book provides basic guidance and reference resources but not step-by-step processes for doing land research or filing a prospecting claim.

Regardless of whether you decide to prospect on public land or stake your own claim, you'll need to find out if there are restrictions on gold extraction methods. We'll provide details about these restrictions and resources that help you stay current, and we suggest joining an active gold prospecting club that can help you interpret and validate your research.

In this book, we focus on gold extraction methods and equipment relevant to South Dakota, Wisconsin, and Minnesota and primarily for beginner to intermediate hobbyist prospectors. This book doesn't cover lode mining because of the major cost (probably in excess of $1 million) of obtaining permits, purchasing industrial equipment, and setting up and running such an operation. Therefore, we strictly cover placer gold. Additionally, we only cover the basics of gold processing (see the Lapidary Arts chapter) because smelting and metalworking for jewelry-making are activities that only a small percentage of hobbyists perform, as these are considered advanced skills.

Gold extraction and processing operations are significantly labor intensive. Once pay dirt (a viable source of placer gold) has been identified, you need to bring in your extraction tools, equipment, and even water if there isn't a reliable source nearby; this might be over a significant distance and change in elevation from where you park your vehicle. You may also need to carry excavated pay dirt a fair distance to your primary processing equipment and your water source, before processing the pay dirt down to concentrate and hauling your equipment and gold concentrate back to your vehicle for final processing and concentration at home. An ATV or even a sturdy wagon can provide a real advantage, but even if you don't have either of these, you need to be in reasonably good physical condition. More importantly, you must enjoy outdoor physical activity. The notable exception to this level of physical exertion is metal detecting for gold nuggets; this might still entail a fair amount of hiking and climbing, but there's no heavy equipment or water to be toted to and from your hunting spots.

This might all sound a bit overwhelming, especially if you've watched videos and TV shows that depict large-scale mining and extraction operations. But don't worry, because even in today's times, simple works best. In fact, the beginning gold prospector will only have to spend about $200 for equipment, and that might be all they'll ever need! And this basic equipment is light and portable, easing the labor of hauling it in and out of your work area. Like all hobbies, take it step-by-step, because the simple and basic tools and processes will continue to be useful even if you ultimately "graduate" to bigger and better equipment.

# GOLD TYPES

There are several distinct forms or types of gold. The first (in host) requires hard rock mining, which is not taught in this book. The remaining four are all types or forms of placer gold.

**Gold in host quartz:** Nearly all gold is formed within veins of quartz. It can be tiny flakes of gold that are widely interspersed, in large crystal formations, or in highly concentrated pockets. Extracting gold from host quartz is an intense process. First, extensive drilling and core sampling is done to identify veins of quartz that are sufficiently rich in gold. Next, the material is mined, and then it has to be crushed and chemically processed to separate gold from quartz and other minerals.

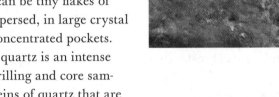

**Nugget:** Gold nuggets are large concentrations of gold that have weathered out of host quartz. An average nugget is less than 1 gram (there are roughly 31 grams in 1 troy ounce). The largest gold nugget known to be found in the Black Hills is approximately 5¼ troy ounces, and it was found in 2010. (There was a larger nugget claimed to be found in 1929, but the origin of that nugget is disputed.) Most prospectors consider anything larger than ½ ounce to

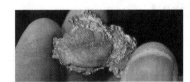

be a lifetime treasure that they would be sorely pressed to part with!

**Flake:** Flake gold is very flat and was formed that way in the host quartz or by natural weathering processes. Gold flakes are micro-thin and will actually float around in moving water, so one must be careful when panning because gold flakes can easily float out of the pan.

**Fine gold:** Fine gold (sometimes called "gold fines") is small granules similar in size to coarse-grained sand. This is the most common form of placer gold that you will find in the Black Hills. Therefore, most of the detailed processes we cover are focused on fine gold. The very finest gold is sometimes referred to as "flour gold," which is so small that when it's dry it is almost powdery, like flour. It's the most difficult gold to process and requires multiple rounds of "concentration" to separate it from very fine dirt and sand. The process also requires specialized equipment, such as a spiral concentrator or a miller table, and it is generally beyond the range of beginning gold prospecting.

## IMPOSTERS

There's a famous saying in gold prospecting: "There are a lot of things that look like gold, but gold doesn't look like anything else."

Pyrite is the most common imposter, hence its nickname of "fool's gold." Here are some testing and identification methods:

- Density is the primary distinguishing factor; gold is much heavier than pyrite, so gold will be left at the top rim of your gold pan, while pyrite will have either washed out or perhaps be left in with the black sand (fine granules of magnetite and hematite).

- If there is a larger pyrite chunk, it can be inspected to see if it has the cubic crystal structure that is peculiar to pyrite and not gold.

- Gold is a much brighter and distinctive yellow-gold color, and it's more lustrous than pyrite.

Mica flakes will also get your attention, but mica is a much less troublesome imposter because it is extremely light and will quickly wash out of the gold pan or any other gold concentration device.

## GOLD PROSPECTING REGIONS

In the Midwest, there are a few regions with active gold prospecting. If you want to try to find enough gold to cover your "hobby expenses," and possibly even make a bit of profit, western South Dakota is where you'll need to look. However, as with most of the gems and minerals in this book, gold prospecting in Minnesota and Wisconsin is a serious hobby, even if not a profitable one, and there are many modern-day prospectors in northwestern Wisconsin and north-central Minnesota that regularly get gold in their pans and sluice boxes. There are even occasional "specimen finds" to be had, such as finding gold-containing host rock at gravel pits that are being panned or sluiced for placer gold.

## THE BLACK HILLS OF SOUTH DAKOTA

There are too many gold prospecting opportunities to name them all, but this map provides some "hot zones" that have historically produced high volumes of placer gold. Additionally, almost all of the drainage creeks that flow through the Black Hills will provide good "bench gravels" that contain fine gold. (Bench gravel is material found up the valley slope from the stream that was deposited when the stream used to run at that higher level.) Most notably, the Rapid, French, Iron, and Spring Creeks are worthy of exploration—especially in or near the hot zones noted on the map.

**Black Hills Gold Prospecting Hot Zones**

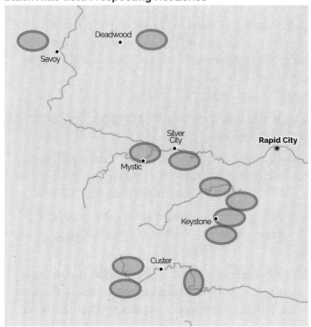

# South Dakota Gold Prospecting Rules and Regulations

There is an abundance of public land where gold can be found in the Black Hills, but it comes with substantial restrictions concerning land use and environmental protection. This is another important reason for joining a club; they have already gone through the needed permitting processes! If you later decide to strike out on your own, the club members can walk you through these sometimes complex and confusing processes step-by-step. The Bureau of Land Management (BLM), part of the U.S. Forest Service, publishes guidance at the link below. We will also provide additional restrictions that are more difficult to find on public websites or documents. After accessing this link, you'll need to select "Gold Panning" and then "Gold Panning & Sluicing." www.fs.usda.gov/activity/blackhills/recreation/rocks-minerals

## Rules and Regulations

- Battery-powered machines are allowed up to 12 volts.

    a. If you acquire and set up a 25-watt solar panel, you can recharge your battery at the site.

    b. Turn off power to your equipment when not using it.

    c. Highbanker and Gold Cube water pumps both can run on 12-volt batteries.

- Any time you are using water "for profit," the limit without a permit is 18 gallons per minute (1,080 gallons per hour).

- Gas-powered engines are generally not allowed in the Black Hills, so we strongly recommend running on battery power. You can request a permit to run a gas-powered engine at the link below. Note that the Black Hills Prospecting Club has such a permit for their claims: denr.sd.gov/des/mm/minepermits.aspx

- No powered suction dredging is allowed, including float dredges; see info at this link: denr.sd.gov/des/mm/minepermits.aspx

- Metal detecting requires a state permit, and there are specific rules and restrictions that are outlined at the link below. Note that the Black Hills Prospecting Club has such a permit for their claims: gfp.sd.gov/metal-detector/

- Regulations state that after "mining operations" have been completed, the land must be restored to its natural condition—as it was before the mining work commenced.

- Off-highway vehicle (OHV) access requires a special permit that is available at the following link, which also provides a free map and links to any current closures or further restrictions, such as for seasonal, weather-related, or other safety and maintenance issues: www.fs.usda.gov/activity/blackhills/recreation/ohv

# MINNESOTA AND WISCONSIN

Small amounts of fine gold can be found in many parts of the upper Midwest, including northern Minnesota, northern Wisconsin, and the Upper Peninsula of Michigan.

## Minnesota's Best-Known Gold Prospecting Region

One area where placer gold is concentrated is south of Minnesota's Lake Vermilion. There was even a mini-gold rush in this area in 1865–1867, but it fizzled out quickly. The areas shown below have a higher concentration of fine gold particulates as assessed by the Minnesota DNR. The best opportunities for finding and recovering gold are along small streams and rivers in these areas. However, these are only starting points for your prospecting, and there haven't been any reports of large placer gold finds by hobby prospectors.

**Minnesota's Best-Known Gold Prospecting Region**

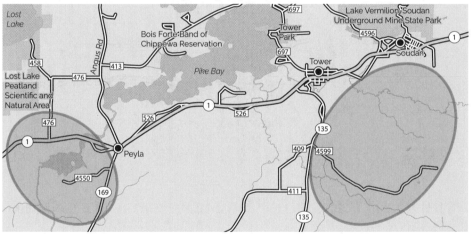

# Wisconsin's Best-Known Gold Prospecting Region

In western Wisconsin, a location of note is near Nugget Lake, along rivers and streams such as Plum Creek, which flows out of the southeastern end of the lake. Nugget Lake is about an hour's drive west of Eau Claire. As of this publication, there is a very active Facebook group (see page 137) with regular postings about prospecting in this area.

**Wisconsin's Best-Known Gold Prospecting Region**

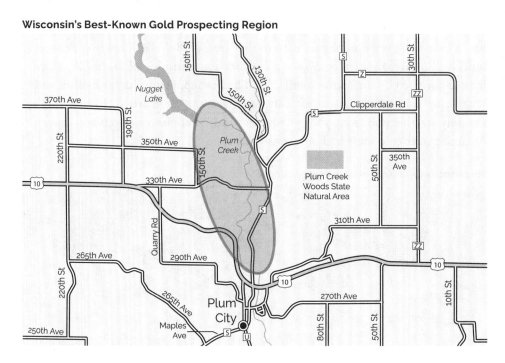

# Minnesota and Wisconsin Gold Prospecting Rules and Regulations

Minnesota and Wisconsin have more-restrictive rules and regulations on state land than South Dakota, and we've noted some of these restrictions below. Because of these constraints, many hobbyists seek out private or county-owned land to prospect and extract gold. This land might have a flowing stream, or sand and gravel pits. One benefit of pits is that they have permits to run mechanical equipment. So if you attain permission to do some gold prospecting at a sand and gravel pit, and you have motorized equipment such as a sluice, ask if they would allow you to use it.

### Minnesota Rules and Regulations

Gold prospecting and recovery are allowed on state lands, but there are many caveats and restrictions. The DNR Recreational Geology webpage provides some details at this link, with key information following:
www.dnr.state.mn.us/geologyrec/index.html

- No permits are required on state lands, but state parks are off-limits.

- Recreational gold prospecting is allowed with handheld, non-mechanical, and non-motorized tools, including gold pans, shovels, and buckets.

- Stream sluices are not allowed, nor are handheld suction dredges or devices.

- Some areas and times, such as trout streams, protected-habitat areas, or spawning season, are off-limits, so you need to check with local area fisheries managers or other DNR representatives to verify if they have any such restrictions in place.

### Wisconsin Rules and Regulations

Wisconsin has less-stringent restrictions regarding recreational gold prospecting than Minnesota, as shown at the following link, with key points noted below. However, their land use restrictions are stricter than Minnesota's: dnr.wi.gov/files/PDF/pubs/wa/WA1504.pdf

- Non-mechanized prospecting and extraction is allowed without a permit, including panning, stream sluicing, and metal detecting.

- Gold collected primarily for sale or profit is considered commercial mining and isn't allowed without a permit.

- Any prospecting and extraction on state-owned land requires a permit from the DNR.

- If you receive a permit, you can only remove 5 pounds of material per day from the site and 50 pounds total per year.

- You cannot prospect or collect materials on the following state-owned properties: state parks, state trails, state recreational areas, wild and scenic rivers as designated by the state, and state natural areas.

# UPPER MIDWEST "SECONDHAND" PLACER GOLD

In addition to the placer deposits near Lake Vermilion and Nugget Lake, there are glacial "redeposits" of placer gold throughout the Upper Midwest, which some hobby prospectors refer to as "re-placer" gold or "secondhand" placer gold, because it was carried from its original location by glaciers and then deposited in glacial till. The best way to find these deposits is through the use of DNR aggregate maps. See page 27 for more information on these maps and how to use them to identify significant deposits of glacial till and both active and inactive sand and gravel pits. Remember that you need permission to hunt on private land; helpful suggestions are provided throughout the Lake Superior Agates chapter.

For gold prospecting and recovery, you'll use these maps a bit differently. Your best opportunities for finding gold in glacial till are in streams that run through the sand and gravel. These streams are great for gold panning! Gravel pits themselves provide some opportunities, if you can secure approval to prospect for gold in them. Focus on the areas beneath the sidewalls of the gravel pit that have been

washed out by rain and snow melt. This photo shows an alluvial fan at the base of a sidewall. This material is the best candidate for digging and testing for fine gold. Since active gravel pits have a water source for their rock-washing operations, you can use some of that water to do test pans or even set up a small processing operation right in the gravel pit. Be sure to inform the pit owners and operators if you decide to do on-site processing!

In addition to the possibility of finding placer gold in Minnesota and Wisconsin gravel pits, there are rare finds of gold still in its host rock. One such example is shown here. This piece was found in a Minnesota gravel pit between Silver Bay and Ely. So if you are having success finding traces of placer gold, you will be well advised to keep an eye out for other stones that have a yellow- or gold-tinted shine!

## PROSPECTING VENUES

The prospecting venues covered in this book are strictly for placer gold, which is gold that has already weathered out of its host quartz. Gold that is still embedded in host quartz veins is known as "lode gold" and can only be extracted through intensive commercial operations. However, it is valuable to know where these lode sources are because they will lead you toward placer gold concentrations.

The illustration below depicts the different hunting venues of interest to hobbyists. In the Black Hills, the greatest concentration of placer gold is in eluvial deposits (material weathered free but still close to its source) and bench deposits, with the latter being generally greater. This goes for all methods of prospecting, including metal detecting. Gold can also be found in the creeks and streams; these have been worked rather extensively, and there are significant restrictions about operating large equipment such as float dredges (which are also quite expensive and require scuba diving equipment and skills), so your best opportunities will come after there has been significant precipitation and runoff. It's also possible to find gold by doing some metal detecting in and around old mine tailing piles, but these have been worked extensively, so we won't cover this hunting venue.

**Gold Hunting Venues**

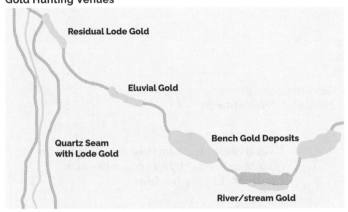

The illustrations here and on the next page provide a good visualization of how to read a river or stream to identify the most probable places where placer gold has "come to rest."

**Gold Deposits in a River or Stream**

**Gold Deposits in a River or Stream**

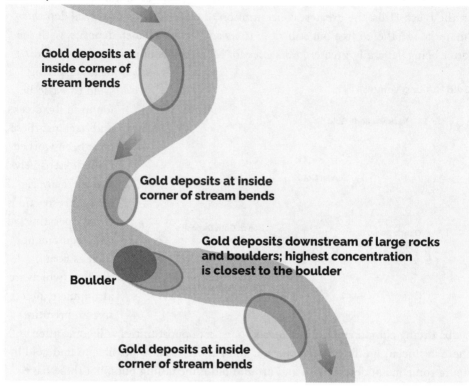

Gold deposits at inside corner of stream bends

Gold deposits at inside corner of stream bends

Gold deposits downstream of large rocks and boulders; highest concentration is closest to the boulder

Boulder

Gold deposits at inside corner of stream bends

# GENERAL PROSPECTING AND HUNTING PROCESS

There are four major phases of hobby gold mining: prospecting, extraction, concentration, and refining (also known as casting). While prospecting is often thought to start with gold panning itself, there is some preliminary research necessary before heading out into the wild with your trusty gold pan. That's not to say that when hiking in an area known to contain placer gold you can't do a couple of "test pans" to see what you find, but be aware that this can be viewed as claim jumping by a legitimate claim owner. Knowing that claim owners have gone through a time-consuming and expensive process to find productive ground and file their claims, you shouldn't be surprised if they become angry or even press charges against you, even for just running test pans. This is especially true if their claims are well marked. Unfortunately, many claims are poorly marked or not marked at all, and there are no consistently applied standards for marking claims. The rule of thumb is that if you see any type of marker, you are well advised to select a different location. Markers could be anything from a PVC pipe that might contain claim details inside to a wooden or metal signpost or stake, which may or may not have a legible notice posted on it.

Due to the time and expense of locating a viable piece of land, filing your claim, and paying annual fees, **we strongly recommend that beginning prospectors join one of the gold prospecting clubs in the Black Hills**. Both the Black Hills Prospecting Club and Northern Hills Prospectors have claims that you can use just by becoming a member of the club. There is still plenty of gold to be found on their claims, and more importantly, you can learn from seasoned experts how to perform almost every process step that we explain before you start buying your own tools and equipment. After you've gained this invaluable experience, you can decide to seek out your own claim if you wish, and club members can guide you through the process of filing and staking your claim. One additional option that we will describe is how to gain approval from private landowners that have mineral-extraction rights on their land that are granted and documented within a "land patent."

## Safety Factors

Here are some essential safety recommendations for beginners and experts alike.

- **NEVER ATTEMPT TO ENTER AN OLD MINE SHAFT, AND DO NOT EVEN STEP CLOSE TO ANY VISIBLE ENTRYWAYS!** The ground in and around mine shafts is notoriously unstable. If the ground were to collapse, you could fall deep into an old mineshaft filled with rocks and timbers. Do not let your curiosity or gold fever get the best of you!

- Never set up a gold prospecting and extraction operation until you have determined that it is not part of a claim, or unless you have written authorization to prospect on someone else's claim or land patent. Even if there are no clear claim markers, you cannot assume the right to work on it. Claim owners might take the law into their own hands if they find you working their claim, or they might have you arrested, facing a hefty fine.

- Gold prospecting and extraction can be hard work. Hiking with heavy equipment, digging, hauling pay dirt, and operating the equipment all require physical labor. Make sure to bring drinking water and nourishing snacks, take periodic breaks, and know when to call it a day—even if you are on a good "paystreak."

- When working on bench deposits, there will sometimes be steep cliffs. Make sure to ensure that the ground is stable, especially any overhanging material.

- You must be ever vigilant for dangerous wildlife, such as snakes or mountain lions, especially considering the remote areas you'll likely be in.

- Plan for the weather, both current and forecast, and for potential storms or other extreme changes. Let someone know where you're going and when you plan to return, and do your prospecting with one or more trusted partners.

# STEP-BY-STEP PROSPECTING AND HUNTING PROCESS

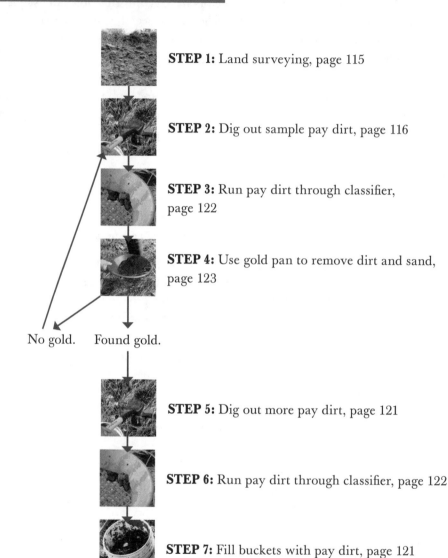

**STEP 1:** Land surveying, page 115

**STEP 2:** Dig out sample pay dirt, page 116

**STEP 3:** Run pay dirt through classifier, page 122

**STEP 4:** Use gold pan to remove dirt and sand, page 123

No gold.     Found gold.

**STEP 5:** Dig out more pay dirt, page 121

**STEP 6:** Run pay dirt through classifier, page 122

**STEP 7:** Fill buckets with pay dirt, page 121

**STEP 8:** Option 1:
Pan the pay dirt, page 123

**STEP 8:** Option 2:
Run pay dirt through sluice, page 125

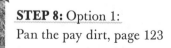

**STEP 9:** Run fine sand through concentration device (for example: Gold Cube), page 127

# Prospecting Phase

To become familiar with the process, it's helpful to outline the most common steps or methods within each of the four major phases of gold mining. For experienced prospectors, some of the steps outlined will be overkill, and some people like to operate in a more spontaneous fashion. But as with any serious hobby, you will attain skills and repeatable success more quickly if you apply this discipline while you're learning the ropes. While others are becoming frustrated and quitting, you'll be hitting your stride and bringing home the gold!

## 1. Land Research to Identify Target Zone

**At home, online, and driving around:**

- Research placer gold claim maps to identify one or more hot zones to explore.
- Review Forest Service and BLM websites to determine any access or use restrictions, including temporary or seasonal closures.

**At the site:**

- Perform a visual "land survey" to see if there are bedrock formations, or signs of ancient river bends that could hold alluvial gold deposits.
- Scout the area to ensure there are no claim markers.
- Identify access points and availability of water at or near the site.
- If there's a stream, identify inner bends with large rocks that might be good places for suction dredging.

**Tools, equipment, reference information:** Local clubs and experts, placer gold claim maps to identify hot zones, detailed physical maps, Forest Service and BLM website information with OHV road and trail maps, access and land use restrictions, etc.

**Results:** One or more possible locations to perform prospecting, along with travel and access information about the sites

## 2. Target Zone Refinement and Mapping

- Perform test pans, metal detecting sweeps (for black sand and small gold nuggets), and suction dredge sampling.
- Record results from around your site in your prospecting log.
- Update notes on accessibility, water availability, etc.
- Verify that there are no claim markers visible.

**Tools, equipment, reference information:** Gold panning/prospecting kit (see page 133), water, physical map, GPS, prospecting log, first aid kit, beverages and nourishing snacks

**Results:** Gold samples, a detailed map of results (positive and negative), site survey of accessibility, water availability, etc.

## 3. Gold Extraction and Processing Plan

- Determine primary methods for gold extraction, such as manual or power sluicing, metal detecting, suction dredging, etc.
- Make a rough outline, including timing, for loading gear, travel, setup activities, extraction, and concentration operations.

**Tools, equipment, reference information:** Forest Service and BLM websites for updated access or use restrictions, including temporary or seasonal closures, and your own site survey and mapping of prospecting results from the previous step

**Results:** List of equipment, tools, and other resources (such as portable water) that will be needed, how you will transport things to and from the site, and a rough time schedule of activities

# Extraction Phase

## 1. Setup

- Pack and haul equipment to site and set up.

**Tools, equipment, reference information:** Extraction and processing plan, gold panning/prospecting kit, sluice box, rocker box, Gold Cube, highbanker power sluice, batteries and solar battery-charging equipment, metal detector, water supply if no nearby streams, prospecting log, first aid kit, beverages and nourishing snacks

**Results:** Equipment set up and operational at claim site

## 2. Pay Dirt Collection and Processing

- Go to your highest prioritized spot on the extraction and processing plan, and dig out sample pay dirt, about three 5-gallon buckets' worth.
- Process the sample pay dirt in a sluice (stream, rocker box, highbanker).
- Use your gold pan to see if you have any gold. If not, pick the next spot on your extraction plan, and dig and sample more pay dirt. If you do find gold, proceed to the next step.
- Dig and process all the pay dirt in your selected spot.
- Put the material into a separate bucket for concentration—**put this bucket in a separate and secure spot so it doesn't accidentally get dumped out!**
- Proceed to the next spot on your extraction and processing plan.

**Tools, equipment, reference information:** Extraction and processing plan, gold panning/prospecting kit, sluice box, rocker box, Gold Cube, highbanker power sluice, batteries and solar battery-charging equipment

**Results:** 75% pure gold concentrate

### 3. Metal Detecting for Nuggets

- Select and mark an area of ground to cover.

- Tune your metal detector, using gold, black sand, and junk samples (see Metal Detecting chapter for more on tuning).

- Work a grid pattern over the selected ground until you've exhausted the selected area.

- You can either "resolve" each hit as you go, stopping to see what you found, or you can put dirt clumps into a 5-gallon bucket as you go and pan it all out at one time. If you choose to resolve hits as you go, a handheld pinpoint detector will come in handy.

**Tools, equipment, reference information:** Extraction and processing plan, metal detector(s), metal detecting permit

**Results:** Gold nuggets and some fine gold pieces

### 4. Suction Dredging

- Use your suction dredge to suction out dirt and water behind large boulders, discharging it into a 5-gallon bucket.

- Periodically pour off excess water so that only dirt is remaining at the bottom of the bucket.

- Once you have a good amount of dirt, do a cleanup with your gold pan or stream sluice.

**Tools, equipment, reference information:** Extraction and processing plan, hand suction dredge, gold panning/prospecting kit, sluice box

**Results:** 65% pure gold concentrate

## Concentration Phase

### Concentration Option 1

- Run your pay dirt through a Gold Cube or other concentration device, such as a bucket concentrator, and place any gold fines, flakes, or nuggets into a vial. It might take you several rounds if you have a large volume of dirt.

**Tools, equipment, reference information:** Gold pan

**Results:** 90% pure gold concentrate

## Concentration Option 2

- If you have a large volume of pay dirt with very fine gold, first run it through a Gold Cube.

- Take the remaining dirt and run it through your gold pan, and place any gold fines, flakes, or nuggets into a vial.

**Tools, equipment, reference information:** Gold Cube, gold pan

**Results:** 90% pure gold concentrate

## Concentration Option 3

- If you are working with very fine or "flour" gold, you can run your pay dirt through a Gold Cube first and then use a gold table or spiral concentrator to extract out the very fine gold particles.

**Tools, equipment, reference information:** Gold table or spiral concentrator

**Results:** 90% pure gold concentrate

## PROCESS DETAILS

First off, it's good to know how commonly each gold recovery method is used and what results you will get for your time, effort, and expense. This table shows approximately what percentage of gold comes from each method we cover in this book. Surprisingly, even in today's modern and technologically advanced times, some gold prospectors never work with any special tools or equipment other than a trusty gold pan!

| Method | % Gold Found |
|---|---|
| Panning | 25 |
| Stream sluicing | 35 |
| Highbanker sluicing | 25 |
| Rocker box sluicing | 5 |
| Suction dredging | 5 |
| Metal detecting | 5 |

The processes that follow are generally in the order that they'll be performed. We introduce gold panning early on, however, because it comes into play often and is a process that prospectors can hone into a fine skill and art.

# Land Surveying

When you find concentrations of smooth and rounded rocks, they are generally from the Tertiary Period, and they suggest the possibility of lode gold that has weathered out into placer gold deposits.

Notice the high concentrations of smooth and rounded rocks.

Since gold is formed in quartz, finding a high concentration of quartz rocks suggests the possibility of placer gold nearby.

"Stepped" bowl formations show the path of old rivers and streams and suggest the possibility of bench deposits.

Bedrock near the bottom of the bowl formations is where placer gold most likely settled when rivers and streams ran at higher levels. This is where we'll be digging for pay dirt in the next process section.

Any of the creeks running through the Black Hills are great places to prospect for gold. Focus on the inner bends of streams and immediately downstream from large rocks and boulders.

The presence of quartz veins is another clue that nearby there might be placer gold that has weathered out of the host rock.

Protruding rows of mica schist "riffles" are a good place for metal detecting. Mica schist is another common gold companion, and placer gold or small gold nuggets can get trapped between the schist layers.

A few pieces of mica schist, which is sometimes found in layers, as shown above. They have a light-metallic glow to them.

There's an endless variety of claim stake markers and no trespassing signage. Sometimes you'll find details inside the marker, such as in a PVC pipe, sometimes they'll be on the sign itself, and sometimes they may have weathered away. From a practical standpoint, you should assume that the claim is still valid and encompasses at least an acre of land around the marker.

## Digging Pay Dirt

You'll make many trips to your processing station—fewer buckets with multiple trips, or multiple buckets with fewer trips. If digging above a solid bedrock formation, begin digging out the topsoil right above the bedrock. Gold always settles on top of the rock, whether it's on dry land or in a stream.

Tightly work the shovel blade against the hard surface because that's where the gold is most likely to be.

Use a crevice tool, such as a long flathead screwdriver, to get the last of the dirt out of both vertical and horizontal crevices. After careful digging, you might even use a stiff-bristle brush to brush dirt into your bucket or onto the shovel blade.

## Classifying

Classifying is the removal of larger-size stones from pay dirt, and it is done before processing pay dirt with a gold pan. It's important to do this because the larger rocks can push gold out of the pan along with dirt and sand. Be sure to look carefully at the rocks before discarding them, as there just might be a nugget in the mix!

Classifying pans come in several different gauges or mesh sizes, and some use a plastic bottom section while others are metal screen.

# Panning

Once the larger rocks are removed, you are ready to begin panning. Because gold is heavier than any other material, it will quickly settle to the bottom of the pan, and the lighter dirt and sediment will rise to the top.

Begin by tilting your pan into the water so that water covers your pay dirt but doesn't fill the whole pan. Raise the pan out of the water, holding it horizontally, and begin to swirl the water around the pan, suspending the lighter material in the moving water. Next, tilt the pan downward to allow some of the water and dirt to spill out of the pan. Carefully scoop up a little more water in your pan, and repeat the process one or two more times.

After doing the process a few times, you can use the technique of gently but firmly rapping the side of the pan with your hand. This helps heavier material like gold and black sand settle to the bottom, allowing lighter material to mix with the water and be poured out.

Occasionally work the remaining material with your fingers to find any larger pebbles and remove them. Remember to be on the lookout for nuggets so that you don't inadvertently discard them!

Keep processing until you are down to black sand and hopefully a couple of gold "colors" in your pan!

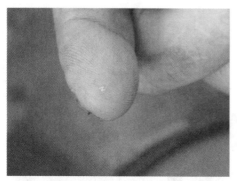

You can use your fingertips, a pair of tweezers, or a snuffer bottle to remove any gold grains and place them carefully into your collecting vial.

To expose very fine gold, you might first need to remove any black sand. Many gold picks have a magnet on the end of them for this purpose.

If prospecting in an area with a lot of gold flakes, consider doing your panning over a large tub instead of in a stream, as flakes tend to float, and they could easily float away downstream.

# Sluicing, Option 1: Stream Sluicing

Non-mechanized stream sluicing with a portable sluice box is perhaps the most widely used method of processing pay dirt in the Black Hills and Wisconsin. These devices are lightweight, and they can easily be carried into remote locations.

The trick is to get them set up so that there is a good flow of water that causes a vigorous rippling action over the metal screen. Usually you'll need to place a couple of large rocks on either side of the sluice box to hold it in place and to channel the water. Remember to put the rocks back as you found them when you are done for the day.

Feed the pay dirt into the sluice gradually, so very fine gold or gold flake doesn't float away.

Break up any clumps of dirt and grass so they don't clog up the flow of water in the sluice.

Gently lift the sluice box out of the stream and place the end into a classifier-and-pan combination. Use at least one bucket of water to rinse the entire sluice box.

Remove the metal screen, roll the underlying mat down, and add water to hand rinse all of the dirt and rock out of the mat. The next step is the panning process.

## Sluicing, Option 2: Mechanized Sluicing

The highbanker mechanized sluice is probably the second-most popular method of processing pay dirt. It can handle vastly greater volumes of pay dirt than a stream sluice, but it also requires more power and water, as well as special permitting.

Equipment needs to be hauled in and out with some kind of motorized vehicle, given the weight and size.

The first thing you need to do is get the machine set up, with water being pumped from a reliable water source, such as a stream or a holding pond.

Just as with the stream sluice, you'll feed in your pay dirt at a slow enough pace that the machine can run without clogging up. The water above the riffles should be moving freely with good rippling action.

After processing all of your pay dirt, it's time for cleanup. You'll have a few more steps than the stream sluice because there are more parts and layers in a highbanker, including the top riffle (metal grate), classifying screen, textured matting, and ribbed matting. All of these need to be removed carefully and rinsed in a classifier-and-pan combination. The classifying screen might contain small gold nuggets, so it should be inspected separately.

The ribbed matting needs to be handled a bit more carefully. This is usually done in a small tub where it is turned inside out and massaged to release all of the dirt, black sand, and (hopefully) fine gold. Most of the water in the tub is poured off after settling for a minute or two, and the remainder is poured into the classifier-and-pan combination.

One additional sluicing option is a rocker box. This non-motorized machine comes into play if you don't have a fast-moving stream and you don't have a permit to run mechanized equipment. It's relatively lightweight and therefore easy to haul into remote locations. You will need a nearby water source and a large tub; this will enable you to pump water into it, and then recycle it.

## Fine Gold Concentration

There are numerous devices and contraptions for concentrating very fine gold. We prefer the Gold Cube because of its simple operation and its ability to capture very fine gold. Quite often this machine is set up at home, instead of hauled to where the pay dirt is. There are three separate levels in this machine that trap fine gold.

Submerge the pump end into your water source. Water will drain into a smaller tub beneath the Gold Cube, and it can be poured back into the supply tub once it's full. This is especially important if you're in a remote location with a limited water supply.

Connect your power source to the pump, in this case a 12V battery. The Gold Cube is now ready for processing.

Gradually feed pay dirt concentrate into the top level, spreading it from side to side to keep the flow even.

Turn off the water supply after you've processed all of your pay dirt concentrate, and empty the top layer into your gold pan. Note that you'll perform this same operation for each of the three layers. About 70–80% of your gold will be in the top layer.

Perform the panning process. Notice the significant volume of black sand and a very large number of gold "colors" in this pan. That's because this was the result of running almost two 5-gallon pails of pay dirt concentrate from the collecting site.

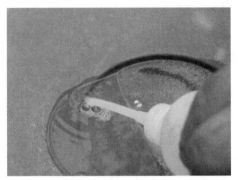
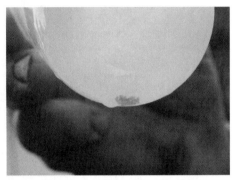

The middle tray from the Gold Cube held no gold, so the first level caught everything! The bottom tray also came out with no gold, so the Gold Cube worked perfectly! If there were any flour gold, it likely would have showed up in levels two and three.

Other methods of final gold concentration include: spiral wheel concentrator, miller table, and bucket concentrator.

## Suction Dredging

Suction dredging involves suctioning small gold particles out of bedrock crevices in rivers and streams. There are many kinds of dredges, but this book will only cover the use of handheld suction tube "dredges." We don't cover float dredges or motorized dredges because of intensive restrictions in South Dakota, Minnesota, and Wisconsin. Additionally, there are few rivers or streams that are large enough or contain enough gold to make them financially feasible.

As shown on pages 111–112, you'll be looking for gold where it "comes to rest," downstream of large rocks along or near the inner bend of a stream. The majority of gold will end up directly behind the rocks and in any crevices immediately downstream from the rocks. Place the nozzle of the suction tube directly behind the boulder, and suction out the dirt and sand. Empty the tube into your gold pan or into a 5-gallon bucket (some have an outflow tube that feeds directly into a bucket), and then continue to work downstream about 1 or 2 feet from the boulder. Once you have a full gold pan or sufficient material in your 5-gallon bucket, use the standard panning process.

## Metal Detecting

Note: Refer to the Metal Detecting chapter for details on selecting a detector for gold prospecting and how to tune your metal detector, along with some basic usage recommendations. Based on your prospecting log, select areas that are good candidates for finding gold nuggets. You must work these areas slowly and methodically using **deliberate and slow sweeps**. A large majority of the nuggets you'll find will weigh less than a gram. Make sure to record your results—positive and negative. Seasoned gold nugget detectors will tell you about finding patches that yielded many good specimens. They'll also tell you of long dry spells.

A great place to do some detecting is anywhere that you've already been digging for bench or eluvial gold. Work the detector in tight against the bedrock and into any crevices that you can angle the head of the detector into.

After getting a good hit and pinpointing the location, dig out a section of dirt

Check your sample to see if you successfully dug out the metallic object that triggered the signal.

Place the chunk of dirt and grass into your gold pan. Remember that most gold nuggets will be smaller than 1 gram, so it's best to just get the dirt into your pan at this point instead of trying to isolate it further. Next, perform the standard panning process.

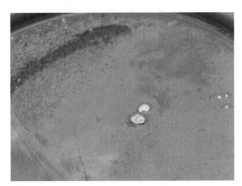

This is considered an **awesome** find.

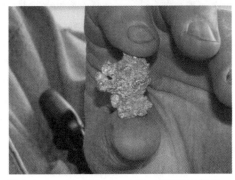

This is considered a **once in a lifetime** find!

You can also try some stream detecting. You'll want to concentrate on inner bends of streams and immediately downstream of large rocks.

## TOOLS AND EQUIPMENT

For each of the major processes, there are specific tools and equipment needed, many of them specifically designed and used for gold prospecting and extraction. In addition, there are tools, devices, machines, and even clothing that are needed or at least strongly recommended. The information that follows covers the majority of equipment that we discuss in this book, but remember that there are always new methods and innovative equipment being introduced. For information on metal detectors, consult the Metal Detecting chapter.

Because one can easily spend thousands of dollars on gold prospecting, extraction, and concentration equipment, we've broken things down into different levels of need. We encourage beginners to start at Level 1 and only begin evaluating items in Levels 2 and 3 once they have developed a basic set of skills and a passion for gold prospecting.

## Need Level 1

- Must have for any kind of gold prospecting
- Total cost: $150 if not doing metal detecting; $750 if doing metal detecting

## Need Level 2

- Highly recommended for processing a substantial volume of pay dirt and gold concentrate, or for covering larger amounts of territory in the case of metal detecting
- Total cost: $1,300 if not doing metal detecting; $2,350 if doing metal detecting

## Need Level 3

- Needed for consolidation of very fine gold and for less common prospecting situations and methods

## General Tools and Equipment (Not Included in Levels 1–3)

- Tall rubber wading boots
- Work gloves and possibly waterproof long gloves for cold weather prospecting
- Sturdy collapsible stools
- Wagon or wheelbarrow
- Shovel
- Hand trowel
- Long-handled flathead screwdriver
- 5-gallon buckets

## Specialty Tools and Equipment

- **Gold panning/prospecting kit:** PROSPECTING PHASE, NEED LEVEL 1; Gold pan (we recommend green plastic pans so that black sand is more visible), classifier pans of different mesh sizes: 1/2", 1/4" (most versatile), 1/12" (very fine gold), prospector's pick, snuffer bottle, black sand magnet, tweezers, loupe or handheld magnifier, specimen collection bottles ($50 total)

- **Crevice tools, scrapers, and stiff-bristle brushes of various sizes:** EXTRACTION PHASE, NEED LEVEL 1; 12-piece crevice mining kit ($20)

  https://www.amazon.com/Crevice-Gold-Picks-3-Brushes-Free-Snuffer/dp/B01FG5FBA2

  A long flathead screwdriver can serve as an adequate crevice tool for beginning prospectors.

- **Sluice box:** EXTRACTION PHASE, NEED LEVEL 1 ($100)

- **Metal detectors:** EXTRACTION PHASE, NEED LEVEL 1 ($600, average price of models listed in Metal Detecting chapter). **Pinpoint handheld detector:** NEED LEVEL 2; Garret Pro Pointer AT ($150)

- **Power supply for mechanized equipment:** EXTRACTION PHASE, NEED LEVEL 2; 12V battery and battery charger–preferably solar ($100–200)

- **Highbanker power sluice:** EXTRACTION PHASE, NEED LEVEL 2; www.goldfeverprospecting.com/gobupohiwijo.html ($850)

- **Gold Cube, 3-stack kit:** CONCENTRATE PROCESSING PHASE, NEED LEVEL 2 ($450)

- **Hand (suction) dredge:** EXTRACTION PHASE, NEED LEVEL 3; X-Stream Hybrid Pro Hand Dredge ($150)

- **Rocker box:** EXTRACTION PHASE, NEED LEVEL 3; Gold Grabber rocker box ($600)

- **Miller table:** CONCENTRATE PROCESSING PHASE, NEED LEVEL 3; Black Magic miller table ($190)

- **Spiral wheel concentrator:** CONCENTRATE PROCESSING PHASE, NEED LEVEL 3 ($295)

## Recommended Gold Equipment Merchants

- Gold Fever Prospecting
- Gold Rush Trading Post
- Keene Engineering
- Gold Fox
- ProLine Mining Equipment
- Royal Manufacturing
- Black Cat Mining
- Amazon.com

# CLAIMS AND LAND PATENTS WITHIN NATIONAL FORESTS

We don't advise that beginning gold prospectors start by filing their own claims. You could easily invest several months and thousands of dollars in this process only to find that your claim has little or no productive pay dirt. You might have watched a popular television series in which even seasoned prospectors made big bets on unproven ground only to go bankrupt. The limited testing they did that showed positive results was only a fluke, a "flash in the pan" if you will. Therefore, we offer the information below only as a rough guide to some of the major steps in the process and some key points of contact.

## Claim-filing Basics

- Must have found documented gold
- Annual renewal of claim rights—current fee is $300
- BLM requires squared-off plats rather than "natural boundaries"
- 20 acres per person for a claim; five people together can get 100 acres
- Must post the corners with appropriate signage
- Use of trail cams to monitor
- "Open to mineral entry" classification of public land needed for mineral extraction
- Websites for researching and filing claims

  www.fs.usda.gov/activity/blackhills/recreation/
  rocks-minerals/?recid=25823&actid=59

  minecache.com

  reports.blm.gov/reports.cfm?application=LR2000

## Land Patent Basics

- Go to the county office or go online and look up ownership.
- Identify Forest Service map notations or shadings as to **"patented/private land."**
- Determine whether the landowner has current mineral extraction rights.
- Contact the owner to request access for prospecting; you might want to offer a percentage of the gold you find.

## Land Patent Example

thelandpatents.com/lands/usfs-0471/map

thelandpatents.com/usa/south-dakota/custer-sd033/township-sd070030s0050e/18/patents

- (GPS coordinates)

- Overview Mining - Black Hills National Forest Mining Patent is a 19-acre land patent in Custer, South Dakota. It is a mineral patent, lode.

- Ownership and use of this patent is overseen by the Bureau of Land Management's South Dakota Field Office. The last action for this patent occurred on August 1, 1944. Information on the patent was last updated on July 19, 2011.

- (Serial number)

- 19 Total Acres

- 014 Stat. 0251.Legal Reference

- Mineral Patent, LodeCase Type

# REFERENCES AND RESOURCES

## Books and Articles

- Ralph, Chris. *Fists Full of Gold: How You Can Find Gold in the Mountains and Deserts*. Published by Chris Ralph, 2010.

- Bohmker, Tom. *Gold Panner's Guide to the Black Hills of South Dakota*. Cascades Mountains Gold, 2006.

- Jensen, Rich. "Prospecting in the Hills." *South Dakota Magazine*, March/April 2017. www.southdakotamagazine.com/prospecting-in-the-hills

- Myers, John. "Eureka! DNR Strikes More Gold Near Lake Vermilion." *Duluth News Tribune*, July 1, 2015

  www.duluthnewstribune.com/news/3777887-eureka-dnr-strikes-more-gold-near-lake-vermilion

- "Finding Minnesota: Gold Prospecting In The Midwest Region" WCCO-TV, Minneapolis, MN, March 27, 2016

  minnesota.cbslocal.com/2016/03/27/finding-minnesota-gold-prospecting-in-the-iron-range/

## Facebook Groups and Prospecting Clubs

- Black Hills Prospecting Club of South Dakota, Rapid City, SD
  www.blackhillsprospectingclub.com
- Northern Hills Prospectors, Lead, SD
  www.facebook.com/NorthernHillsProspectors
- Gold Prospectors of Minnesota and Wisconsin
  www.facebook.com/groups/MNGold/

## Gold Maps

- Rapid City South Dakota Area Map of Gold Claims–HH Engineering
  (Cost of $34)
- Minnesota DNR

  www.dnr.state.mn.us/lands_minerals/mpes_projects/project392.html

  http://minarchive.dnr.state.mn.us/mpes/392/cats_murray_road_south_gold_
  grains_july_2017.pdf

# KEOKUK GEODES

With Keokuk, Iowa, as the hub, the tri-state area of southeastern Iowa, northeastern Missouri, and west-central Illinois is one of Earth's premier geode hunting locales. The incredible diversity of geode "types" and the beauty of crystal and mineral formations bring flocks of avid hunters and collectors from all over the world. Internationally, many museums feature Keokuk geode collections that showcase their extensive variety of mineral inclusions and stunning crystal and mineral displays; and some massive geode specimens weigh over 200 pounds. In fact, the region has become so famous that it's been dubbed "The Geode Capital of the World!" There is even an annual festival at which to celebrate, show, sell, and hunt for Keokuk geodes. The festival is a great time to go on a hunt because some collecting sites are only open to the public during the festival, and there are plenty of experts around to provide you with tips and pointers.

Keokuk geodes formed within dolomite or mudstone in what is known as the Lower Warsaw Formation, which was formed about 300 million years ago. As such, these wonderful gemstones could perhaps better be called "Warsaw geodes," but among most hunters and collectors, they have come to be known as Keokuk geodes. There are several factors that make these geodes so highly sought-after and prized.

Opening a geode is always a thrill because you are the first person to see something that has been hidden away for many millions of years. The astonishing diversity of mineral inclusions and crystal formations to be found in Keokuk geodes makes the reveal that much more exciting, and to this day, people are still finding new types. When we say "types," we are referring to variations in the kinds of mineral inclusions (such as pyrite, calcite, and others), the interior configuration (snowball or multi-chamber, for example), and the color and texture of the outer husk, etc. And along with the seemingly limitless geode types and their combinations comes astounding beauty. Of course, everyone loves the beautiful, sparkling crystals in geodes, but premium Keokuks have the bonus of many colorful, striking, and fascinating "prizes" inside, such as: golden pyrite; well-formed and often strikingly colored calcite crystals, including jet black and soft pink; yellow and blue barite crystals; bright-yellow or deep-red dolomite; cubic quartz crystals; wispy, fine millerite crystals; botryoidal chalcedony formations; silvery marcasite needles or crystals; and so much more.

And then there is their size. There are many the size of a cantaloupe, and some "trophy" geodes can be up to the size of a large pumpkin! Extracting very large geodes from hard rock takes skill and hard work, but there are also some to be found in softer clay layers.

Finally, there is the staggering abundance of Keokuk geodes; it's not a question of whether you will find geodes, but how many geodes you'll find. This makes geode hunting in this region especially appealing to new rockhounds, including children.

Keokuk geodes are abundant within the geographical area shown on the maps in this chapter. By far the most prevalent hunting and collecting sites are commercial fee-based hunting properties. Most long-term and experienced collectors have stated that they spend 95% of their time hunting in these sites, and truly we are fortunate that these site owners and operators offer their properties and services in support of the rockhounding hobby! Each site has its own pricing, but many offer rates such as $25 per 5-gallon bucket of geodes, or a dollar amount per pound. Many of the dig sites are periodically "groomed" to ensure access to new material that yields a good volume of retrievable geode concretions. And sites with river or streambed collecting get natural turnover from rain and flooding.

If you have the time and are willing to do some of your own prospecting, you'll be able to find farm fields, construction sites, and rivers or streams that allow you to hunt for free, provided you have obtained approval to hunt on any private property. But many areas with geodes are off-limits to hunting and collecting, such as Iowa's Geode State Park, which strictly prohibits collecting, and there are laws that prohibit hunting and collecting along public highways and roads. Since the commercial properties have all the known types of Keokuk geodes, and the sites are readily accessible, it's hard to make a case for finding your own places to hunt, especially if you are just getting started.

As such, we'll strictly focus on the commercial sites. Ownership and operation of these can change, but most of the sites we include in this book have been in operation for more than five years. A quick call to the Keokuk Area Chamber of Commerce will provide updated information, including any new sites that have recently opened. This doesn't mean you won't have any prospecting to do, it only means you can concentrate on known hunting locations without the worry of getting approvals. Your focus will be primarily on the types and sizes of geodes that can be found at each, and the hunting and collecting methods at different sites.

## KEOKUK GEODE IDENTIFICATION

**Shape:** Shape is the primary identifying feature of geodes in the rough. They all have a somewhat spherical shape with a bubbly or botryoidal (grape-like rounded bumps) surface. Some with a flatter shape are referred to as "pancake" geodes. The photo below shows a variety of shapes.

**Exterior color:** Exterior color is not a distinguishing feature of geodes. They blend in with the host rock, mud, or clay that they are lodged in and with the surrounding sediment after they have already weathered out. Sometimes they are a bit lighter in color but usually not enough to stand out. The photo above shows some color and texture varieties. The darker-gray specimen is possibly indicative of a red-rind geode variety.

**Size:** Keokuk geodes can be less than 1 inch in diameter—or more than 2 feet! In general, people focus on geodes that are at least 3 inches in diameter, although some of the most beautiful and valuable specimens are less than 2 inches. There are also fewer "solid geodes" among these smaller specimens.

**Density:** Density is a good indicator of whether there will be nice crystal structures inside a geode. A solid geode weighs about 50% more than a geode of the same size with a nice crystal cavity. If you are paying for geodes by weight or by the bucket, or if you have a long way to haul your geodes before opening them, you might decide to forego geodes that feel heavy in proportion to size.

Experienced collectors have a keen sense of this density, and they can usually predict whether a geode is a "solid," with less chance of nice crystals inside. While many of the solids are still interesting and pretty inside, they can't compare to geodes that feature nice crystal displays and mineral inclusions.

**Noise:** Loose crystals can sometimes be heard when shaking geodes. This is an instant clue that the geode is not solid and that it has crystal formations. These geodes are nicknamed "rattlers." Note that when opening very lightweight geodes or rattlers, you'll want to apply pressure very slowly, so as not to shatter the geode.

# KEOKUK GEODE TYPES AND FEATURES

More than 25 mineral compounds have been identified in Keokuk geodes, with chalcedony, calcite, and quartz being the most common. There is an almost limitless variety of combinations and configurations to be found in Keokuk geodes, and new types are still being found today. Here are some of the most common types and some of the more unusual and beautiful varieties.

**Quartz crystals:** The most common type of geodes are those with quartz crystals. These two specimens have wonderful large crystal points and a variety of color schemes, from crystal clear to caramel to citrine yellow.

**Snowball quartz crystal clusters:** Snowballs are (somewhat) spherical clusters of quartz crystals. If this specimen had been sawed open, instead of broken open, it might have shattered the crystal clusters.

**Iridescent brown calcite and secondary white calcite crystals:** One stunning and beautiful combination is of bright-white quartz crystals over the top of a lining of brown calcite crystals.

**Large, clear calcite crystals:** Calcite crystals can be distinguished from quartz crystals by their larger and sometimes rhombohedral shapes.

**Rhombohedral calcite crystals:** The calcite rhombohedrons in this example are larger and more white in color than the quartz crystals, which show some oxidization.

**Botryoidal chalcedony:** The botryoidal (grape-like) crystals have "ingested" some kaolinite, so they are opaque rather than clear or translucent.

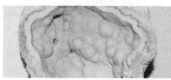

**Sphalerite:** The top half of this geode shows the silvery-black sphalerite crystal, with pink "dogtooth" calcite crystals. The bottom half shows sphalerite nestled in a set of spiky dolomite crystals. While this geode is close to solid, it does have these wonderful mineral inclusions. This shows that there is some risk to leaving behind possibly solid geodes.

**Red-rind:** Red-rind geodes have white and rose-colored druzy quartz linings (fine, sugar-like crystals of quartz), and there is a bit of agate-type pattern formation visible on the interior lining.

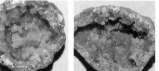

**Blue-rind:** Blue-rind geodes have steel-blue druzy quartz crystals and interior lining. They don't exhibit as much of the agate-type pattern on the inner lining as the red-rind geodes do.

**Pink dogtooth calcite crystals:** Pink dogtooth calcite crystals are surrounded by bright-white quartz crystals.

**Pseudocubic quartz:** These pseudocubic crystals have "ingested" some kaolinite, so they are opaque rather than clear or transparent.

**Quartz and dolomite:** The spiky crystals on the top end are dolomite, and the larger and clearer crystals throughout are quartz.

**Marcasite and kaolinite:** These fine needle inclusions with protruding needles from the main crystal stalk are marcasite. The white powder is kaolinite; it's in a pocket of spiky dolomite crystals that have "ingested" some of the kaolinite, making them milky and nearly opaque.

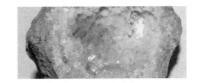

**Brown calcite crystals:** This example shows more of a caramel to citrine color scheme.

**Dolomite rosebud crystals:** In the first photo, gorgeous pink dolomite rosebud crystals are surrounded by bright-white quartz crystals. The second photo is of a very large geode with a wild array of ferroan (iron-bearing) dolomite rosebud crystals.

**Barite crystals:** These two geodes (first photo) formed connected to each other. We carefully sawed away a portion of each geode to better expose the interiors. One geode features ferroan dolomite, and the other contains translucent white barite crystals (see closeup in second photo).

**Ferroan dolomite:** Gorgeous ferroan dolomite crystal clusters and branches are shown here. They are rather delicate, so handle with care. This geode was cracked open first, and then the jagged face was gently sawed away for better presentation.

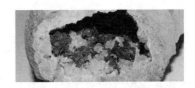

**Pyrite flecks and citrine-colored crystals:** There are tiny pyrite flecks in this geode, and some have partly dissolved, resulting in the amber coloration on the quartz crystals. Most experts say there isn't any true citrine mineralization in Keokuk geodes, but rather it's an oxidization that presents as citrine, as in this example.

**Kaolinite:** Kaolinite is a bright-white mineral compound often found as a fine powder in other geode types, and it is sometimes ingested or infused into quartz, chalcedony, and dolomite crystals. This example shows a solid mass of kaolinite.

**Solid:** Some people find solid geodes interesting and beautiful in their own right, while others discard them or use them as landscaping or garden rocks. It's good to keep a few of these with you when hunting and collecting, as an example of the perceived weight and density of a solid.

**Very large to massive:** It took two people working together for six hours to extract this mostly intact 140-pound specimen from hard rock at St. Francisville Geodes. The crystal configurations and clusters are breathtaking.

# KEOKUK GEODE PROSPECTING REGIONS

While Keokuk geodes can be found within a radius of up to 70 miles from Keokuk, Iowa, the productive hunting range is illustrated in the map below (see page 162 for a map of commercial collecting sites). There are other hotspots in the region, but rest assured that you'll find plenty of premium geodes within the range shown. As you gain more experience with Warsaw Formation geodes, you'll likely explore the boundaries of the hunting range to find some of the more unique varieties. Keokuk is about a 5-hour drive from Chicago, 6½ hours from Minneapolis, and 3 hours from St. Louis.

The main exposures of geode-bearing rock are located within an ancient deposition of dolomitic limestone known as the Lower Warsaw Formation, typically in or alongside streambeds that are tributaries of the Mississippi River. The geodes found loose in creek beds have weathered out of rock within the Lower Warsaw Formation, and some traveled a substantial distance downstream.

**Keokuk Geode Prospecting Regions**

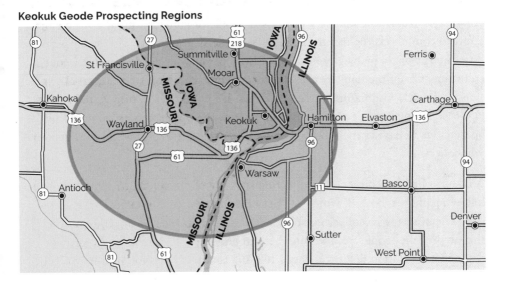

# GENERAL PROSPECTING AND HUNTING PROCESS

For ease of access, the majority of Keokuk geode hunters confine their time and effort to commercial collecting sites. Most of the site operators offer their properties and services primarily because of their passion for geode hunting and collecting. Given the liability risk of letting people climb on steep and rocky hillsides and work with hammers and pickaxes, it's important to respect their rules and their property. They make little money for the opportunities they provide, so be gracious in paying them fairly for the fun, excitement, and wonderful geodes you collect.

A couple of active "mines" (as collecting sites are often called) are featured in the following photos, both of which are periodically groomed to expose new material. The mines have collecting rules, such as not breaking open geodes at the site—to prevent people from leaving behind halves of solid geodes. We provide detailed information below on pages 162–164 that will help you decide which of the commercial sites are best suited to your personal interests, physical abilities, and the kinds of tools you'll need for excavation and collecting. Some sites have a few tools available for you to use or that you can purchase. Many tools can be acquired at hardware or home improvement stores. Some of the sites go so far as to excavate new material that yields a large number of intact geodes, so you can pick by hand without digging or rock chipping.

Start by orienting yourself to the landscape of the commercial geode collecting sites, such as working in water, on steep hillsides, on hard rock surfaces, etc. This will help you narrow your search to areas that might have the geode types

you are most interested in and let you see the relative difficulty of extracting the geodes. It's been observed that plain quartz and dolomite geodes are typically found in brown rock layers, whereas geodes with some of the more exotic and beautiful mineral inclusions are often found in gray rock layers that are a layer beneath the brown layer. But take this as an anecdotal rule of thumb. In the photo below, you can see a faint, wavy gray layer sandwiched between brown to sandy-colored layers. Often the gray layer is much more pronounced, and the geodes will also have a gray outer rind, or husk.

Once you've selected a site, these tips will improve your experience and your results. First, pace yourself in terms of which geodes you decide to keep. Fewer than half of Keokuk geodes contain nice crystal structures, so forego collecting geodes that feel heavy or dense and therefore are probably "solids," especially if you are being charged by the pound or by the bucket. But make sure to understand and comply with site rules. We suggest having several comparison pairs handy so that you can judge your finds against them. Each pair would have a heavier solid and a lighter-weight geode with a nice crystal cavity. You may want pairs of different sizes, such as 2 inches, 4 inches, and 6 inches in diameter. On average, solid geodes weigh about 50% more than geodes with nice crystal cavities.

Another important consideration is that while finding a huge "trophy" geode can be quite a thrill, keep in mind that extracting these huge geodes intact takes a considerable amount of stamina, patience, and skill. It can easily take 4–8 hours to remove a monster geode! And there is no guarantee that you'll get the geode out in one or even two pieces, nor that it will contain a beautiful crystal display inside. As an example, the photo sequence below shows a stunning 5" diameter geode that was in hard rock. Unfortunately, after about a half hour of careful work with a pickaxe, plus hammer and chisel for close-in work, the geode shattered. Note the very thin outer rind; this geode would probably weigh about one-third of what a solid geode of the same diameter weighs.

## Safety Factors

- **Distance:** Since you'll often be working with tools like picks and hammers, it's important to maintain a safe distance of at least 8 feet between yourself and other hunters. One swing of a pick or sledge could result in traumatic injuries from flying rock chunks or being struck by the tool itself.

- **Eye protection:** It's essential that you use high-quality protective glasses or goggles when you are working with picks and hammers. You might even consider wearing a face shield, since flying rock shards can strike you anywhere.

- **Earplugs:** Believe it or not, working around a lot of people doing pick and hammer work on hard rock can be almost deafening. A simple pair of earplugs will help you avoid a pounding headache after a long day of geode hunting and extraction.

- **Surroundings:** Some geode hunting venues have steep rock walls, and ledges that overhang where you might be chiseling and hammering. Ask yourself whether the geodes in precarious settings are worth the risk of having large rocks fall on your head or body. Most of the time you'll be able to find geodes in less risky settings, but if there's a significant trophy geode you are intent on digging out, be sure to proceed extra cautiously, and have a spotter, in case there is a cave-in or rock slide.

- **Water:** Geode extraction can be hard work, so make sure to take regular breaks and stay hydrated. On hot summer days, you should move to a shady area periodically and take a sustained break. Finally, remember that whatever you collect needs to be carried back to your vehicle, so you need to save some energy for your return trip.

- **Weather:** Weather can change quickly. Plan ahead by getting a current forecast, and then regularly monitor the sky throughout the day. Don't wait until the last minute to stop hunting and head to shelter.

## PROCESS DETAILS

There are several hunting modes for Keokuk geodes. Many of the commercial sites feature all of the modes that follow, while others only have one or two primary modes. Details for each site are provided after this section. Each of the methods below is assigned a "difficulty factor," ranging from 1 (easy and minimally labor intensive) to 5 (very difficult and labor intensive).

**Harvesting:** This is by far the easiest collecting mode, with a **Difficulty Factor of 1**. It is simply picking up rocks that have already been weathered or dug out of the host rock and that show typical geode exterior characteristics. Some sites perform periodic excavation and "grooming" that results in geodes being dislodged intact. While this is the easiest mode, take note that in some hunting locations, the geodes you see lying around are ones that have already been deemed "solids" by previous hunters. If you're just getting started, it's worth keeping a few of these geodes to give you a feel for which ones are likely to be solid, but don't fill up your collecting bucket with them!

The process simply involves identifying piles of broken rock material, with a focus on newly broken-out rocks and clay. You can usually tell if people have already been climbing around and digging in the piles by spotting footsteps in the softer material. Start by carefully inspecting the visible material, and remember to think small, since many of the smaller geodes have nice crystal cavities, and they won't fill up your buckets so quickly. After you've scanned the top layer, you can start to move some of the larger rocks to expose more of the material underneath. You just might uncover a very large geode with hardly any work at all!

Harvesting geodes from rock piles at this recently groomed site was a lot of fun. There's a nice baseball-size geode already broken out and ready to "harvest." We scooped up about 40 geodes in a half hour and then headed for the geode cracking table.

After spotting several large-diameter cavities (8 to 12 inches) left from geodes already extracted, we decided to work the area a little farther down. The combination clay-and-rock wall turned out to be very productive! We dug out three very large geodes in a matter of about 20 minutes, using the combination of tools shown. If this had been hard rock, we'd have spent several hours getting these big geodes out intact.

**Clay wall digging:** Digging in clay walls is somewhat strenuous, with a **Difficulty Factor of 3**. You'll be working with a shovel and a pickaxe. Use your shovel to remove top layers of loose material, keeping a lookout for loose geodes that have already weathered out. Once you get down to harder material, be sure to slow down and be less aggressive, so as not to strike hard against a geode and shatter it. Once you spot a rounded nodular formation, you can test with your shovel to see if the material is loose enough to get behind it and pry the geode loose. But don't exert too much pressure if the geode is lodged in tightly. At this point you can use your pickaxe to work all around the exterior of the geode, breaking up the surrounding material. Or you can work more cautiously, with a mini sledge-hammer and Gad Pry Bar or chisel to break up the surrounding material.

**Hard rock geode excavation:** Extracting geodes from rock is the most difficult collecting mode, with a **Difficulty Factor of 4 (rock walls) to 5 (flat rock surface)**. The following general process is recommended. If you are working on a particularly large nodule, proceed with extra patience and caution, so as not to shatter the geode. Experienced geode hunters have reported taking several hours to remove very large specimens!

If working on a tall rock wall with ledges and overhangs, take some time to assess risks of rock falls or slides. You'll be tempted to dive right in when you see a significant number of geodes protruding, but **take heed that falling rocks can cause severe head and body injuries**. Look for a spot that is a safe distance of at least 8 feet from other geode hunters. This is common courtesy, and you can politely remind others of this safety rule of thumb if they arrive after you've started working. Before beginning any work, put on your safety glasses, and also put in earplugs in situations when you and others will be doing a lot of noisy work with hammers and chisels.

Scan the surface for protruding geode nodules. If you spot one or more, then move to the next step. But if there aren't any visible nodules at the surface, you'll have to do some sledgehammer and pick work to get started. Start with the sledgehammer to loosen some rock, and then work with the pickaxe to break the rock down farther. You can also work with a Gad Pry Bar and a mini sledgehammer; drive the pry bar point into hard rock about 6 to 12 inches, and then work it side to side. You might get lucky and have some geode nodules just pop out (like the small geode shown in the third photo on page 153), but after you're done, you'll start to see nodules embedded in the hard rock.

If any of the geode nodules are already somewhat loose (visible cracks or space between the geode and the host rock), then carefully insert the chisel head or pry bar head into the cracks, and gradually drive them into the rock. Stop frequently to assess whether the geode is coming loose and where you need to do the most work to get the nodule to come free.

If the geode is tightly "fused" into the hard rock (as in the example above), and if you are confident in your skills, you can switch to a pickaxe. If you aren't confident with a pickaxe, you can skip this step, especially if it's a very large geode that you are keen on removing intact. It's usually best to start by striking the host rock about 3 inches beneath the geode, which might even cause the geode to pop out. After several strikes beneath the geode, make multiple strikes about 3 inches above and also to the sides of the geode, just to loosen things up.

Each time you shift your striking position, stop to assess whether the geode is coming loose. Also, watch for any opportune cracks that are created, allowing you to use a chisel or pry bar to lever the geode free. We hit this geode lightly, and a portion of the outer rind broke open, so we stopped and switched to the chisel and mini sledgehammer.

Once you've done all you can with a pickaxe, and the geode isn't coming free, begin working with the chisel and mini sledgehammer or a combination hammer pick. If you are working with a chisel, you will need to work all around the perimeter of the exposed geode surface, gradually removing layers of the host material. For a baseball-size geode, it might take you 10–20 minutes, but very large nodules can take hours, and they'll test your stamina and patience. Note: Add about 50%

more time for geodes in a horizontal hard rock surface. Keep in mind that these treasures were formed about 300 million years ago, so it's worth your time and patience to work them out with great care!

The geode we just extracted has a second geode attached on the opposite end. (We featured this geode earlier in this chapter on page 145.) Because both of the geodes had exposed cavities, we decided to use a lapidary saw to open them up. One holds a glorious display of ferroan dolomite leafy crystals, and the other has large and well-formed clear barite crystals.

**River and stream hunting:** This is an enjoyable and relatively easy collecting mode with a **Difficulty Factor of 2 (gravel bar hunting) to 3 (hunting in the water).** In rivers and streams within the Lower Warsaw Formation, heavy rains, flooding rivers, and fast-moving currents can erode the rock walls, freeing many geodes from the host rock. As always, when hunting along rivers and streams, be respectful of deep water and strong currents, and remember that subsurface currents can be hidden by calmer surface conditions.

Gravel bar picking involves methodically walking gravel bars and searching for whole or already open geodes. On our hunt, we found some amazing specimens that were already open.

Two of the three geodes found in the middle photo are already broken open. It's impossible to miss the geode in the photo on the right!

Streambed picking is more difficult because of moving water, and most geodes are covered with algae or mud. You'll need a good pair of waterproof wading boots or sturdy water shoes. The geodes we found were pretty easy to spot. Many times, you need to dig around in the muck to feel for the rounded shapes of geodes, but it sure beats hard rock work, especially on a hot, sunny day!

 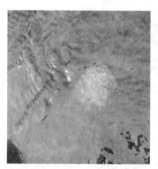 

When there are small ledges or waterfalls in the river or stream, a great place to look is just beneath the drop-off. Notice the nice-size geode we found just beneath the small waterfall.

Hunting along the banks of creeks and streams is another relatively easy and quite productive method for finding geodes in loose dirt, just waiting to be picked. We found a nice softball-size specimen in the dirt behind some overhanging roots.

Here are a couple of the already-open geodes we found; they were cleaned up with a good soapy water scrub and then a soak in Iron Out (more details on these cleaning methods are provided on page 160).

## OPENING GEODES

Cutting geodes open with a rock saw can damage protruding crystals (such as snowball crystal formations), ruin delicate mineral inclusions, and coat the interior of the geode with rock saw oil. There are some situations where you might still choose to use a saw, such as when the geode has already been broken partially open. However, we strongly recommend using pipe cutter tools (the preferred method, but you need to buy the pipe cutter), or using a hammer and a flat chisel (cheaper, but much more difficult and a risk of not getting a clean break).

For the pipe cutter or chisel methods, **put on your safety glasses** and a pair of durable work gloves. Work on a hard, flat surface, such as a heavy workbench or on hard ground, but not directly on the concrete or asphalt of your garage floor or driveway—first put down an old board, a piece of plywood, or even a few layers of cardboard to reduce the risk of harming those surfaces with an errant chisel or hammer blow.

To break geodes open with a flat chisel and hammer, score the geode all the way around its circumference by tapping firmly in one spot and then slowly moving all the way around the circumference of the geode. You need to make visible indentations as you move from position to position. Note that you might need to go around two or three times before the geode breaks open.

Pipe cutters come in various styles and sizes, and there are different processes for each type. We cover each of the types and associated methods below. We also provide pricing for each kind of cutter if you purchase them new. You can also check eBay, pawnshops, or other places that sell used tools to see if you can find one at significant savings. Also, you might consider purchasing one together with other geode hunters, since you don't need it for the hunting process itself. Some of these tools can be purchased on Amazon, but for others you'll need to go to a hardware or home improvement store.

## Pipe Cutters

**Three-wheel pipe cutter:** Ridgid 32820 Model 2-A, .25"–2" ($120); We don't generally recommend a 3-wheel pipe cutter because it doesn't apply pressure as consistently as a 4-wheel and causes more uneven breaks or shattering of geodes. But it can cut smaller geodes than 4-wheel models, and it's still better than a hammer and chisel.

**Four-wheel pipe cutter:** Ridgid 32870 Model 42-A, .75"–2" ($165). Four-wheel cutters provide an even distribution of cutting pressure, and they're super easy to use. Open up the cutting jaws to a little larger than your geode, and then place the geode inside and tighten slowly until the wrench holds the geode firmly. Move the geode around as needed to ensure that its being held firmly, with

about half of the geode on each side of the cutting wheels. Then gradually tighten the wrench until you hear a popping sound and you can see that the geode has been cracked open. To your delight, you can now see the treasure that nature created many millions of years ago.

**Ratcheting pipe cutter:** Ridgid 69982, 1.5"–6" ($700), Wheeler Rex 490, 1.5"–6". The ratcheting pipe cutter can break open geodes up to about 8 inches in diameter (even though they are advertised to cut up to a 6-inch pipe). Lay the chain out flat on your hard surface. Place the geode on the chain along the imaginary line where you want to crack the geode, usually into equal halves. Pull the

chain tight, and hook the nearest pin in the chain into the receptor socket. Manually tighten the chain using the handle, making sure the geode is secured in the position you desire. Then begin using the ratchet to gradually tighten the chain until you hear a popping sound and see a crack all around the geode. If you aren't getting enough pressure to crack the geode open, you might need to tighten the chain another link or two. If this isn't enough to do the trick, you can try giving the chain a few taps with a hammer, but if that fails, you'll probably need to resort to the hammer and chisel method.

**Single-stroke soil pipe cutter:** Ridgid 286 Wheeler Rex 590-8, 1.5"–6" ($500–$600). A single-stroke pipe cutter can break open geodes up to about 8 inches in diameter (even though they are advertised to cut up to a 6-inch pipe). While this is a popular tool for breaking open geodes, we prefer using a ratcheting chain pipe cutter for large geodes because it allows you to increase pressure more gradually. With the single-stroke cutter, it's best to work with two people, one to hold the geode in place and the other to squeeze the handles closed. With the second person holding the sides of the geode (wearing safety glasses), and the lower pipe handle lying flat on the ground, push the top pipe handle down until the geode opens. As with the ratcheting cutter, if you aren't getting enough pressure to crack the geode open, you might need to tighten the chain another link or two.

# CLEANING GEODES FOR DISPLAY

## Exterior Washing

**It's best to wash the exterior of your geodes before cracking them open**, since it's easier to grip and hold the whole geode while scrubbing, and there's less risk of damaging delicate interior crystals. Fill a wash bucket, washtub, or kitchen sink (lined with a rubber mat to avoid scratching your sink) with hot water and some dish detergent. Gently place the geodes into the water, let them soak for an hour or so, and then scrub them with a household scrub brush and then rinse. You can also use a pressure washer if the scrubbing process doesn't clean the exterior to your satisfaction.

## Interior Washing and Stain Removal

Once your geode is open, you can use a soft-bristle toothbrush to clean the interiors. However, be aware that some of the mineral inclusions are quite fine and delicate, so if you have any doubt about whether scrubbing them will cause damage, then leave them as is. Many geodes exhibit oxidation staining that you may want to remove for display. Sometimes this staining provides unique and beautiful coloration, such as a citrine yellow/orange caused by oxidation. If you decide to clean your geodes with any of the commercial products on the next page, be advised that they all contain powerful chemicals that require safe handling and use, and they have the potential to interact with and ruin the unique minerals inside the geode. Therefore, we suggest that you use the chemical cleaning method sparingly. **Read the labels carefully, and adhere to the manufacturer's instructions!**

There are three commercial products that can be used to remove the staining you'll find in some geodes: Iron Out powder, muriatic acid, and Bar Keepers Friend. We strongly recommend Iron Out, because it is the least dangerous and also the least likely to destroy any of the mineral inclusions in your geodes. It takes the longest to work and is less aggressive than the other two options, but always use this as your preferred interior geode cleaning solution.

You need to be in a well-ventilated room or preferably outside. Start with a plastic container with a tight-fitting lid, such as a storage bin. Fill the container about half full with hot water, and then add 3–5 capfuls of Iron Out for every gallon of water; use a stirring stick to mix and dissolve the powder. Wearing rubber gloves, carefully place your geodes in the water. Place the lid on the container, and close it tight. Let the geodes soak for 24–48 hours, checking their progress about every 12 hours and (using rubber gloves) removing any pieces that you are satisfied with, especially any with unique mineral inclusions. As you remove finished pieces, rinse them in lukewarm water and place them in a separate bucket with light soapy water for about 24 hours. One last rinse and your geodes are ready for display! Note that some people will reuse the Iron Out solution if they have multiple batches of geodes to soak. Usually you'll want to add more Iron Out, but if you aren't in a hurry, you can just put your geodes in the solution and see how things turn out after a couple of days.

## COMMERCIAL COLLECTING SITES

This section provides details for six of the most popular sites. Some things in common at most sites:

- Opening and discarding geodes at the site is strictly prohibited.

- Prices vary but usually start at around $25 for a 5-gallon bucket full of geodes.

- Most sites are by appointment, whether for individuals or groups, and some sites won't open unless there is a minimum number of people in the group. **It's always best to call ahead** to make sure the site is open and the operator knows you are coming.

- If you have a large enough group, the site owner might do some "grooming" to expose new material for hunting; it never hurts to ask!

- Most of the sites open up sometime in April and close in October.

- Some sites have food for sale if there will be a group, or during Geode Fest.

- Most sites don't have tools available, so you need to supply your own.

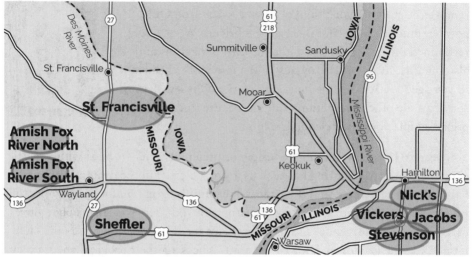

## (Johnny) Vickers Geode Mine

511 S 9th St, Hamilton, IL; 319-795-1219

www.facebook.com/Railroad-creek-Vickers-Geodes-225974610803128

- **Difficulty level:** Easy to medium. Rock wall is periodically "groomed," with loose geodes and easily visible nodules that can be removed with shovels, picks, and chisels. There are also geodes in and along the creek bed, many of which have already been broken open.
- **Accessibility:** Parking area is right at the mine site, so no significant walking
- **Quantity, variety, size:** Good variety of small to medium geodes and some very large geodes
- **Other notes:** If you come in a group or during Geode Fest, the owner will do some "grooming" to expose new material; there are a few "primitive" campsites.

## (Randy at) St. Francisville Geodes

RR 2, Box 33, (Hwy 27 and Rt B) Revere, MO; 660-754-6361

randkfireandice.com

- **Difficulty level:** Medium to difficult. Some ground/surface geodes; significant rock wall digging, especially for very large geodes; no creek or riverbed.
- **Accessibility:** Uphill walk to dig site
- **Quantity, variety, size:** Unique and rare geodes, with large and giant geodes to be found—extracting these monsters can take many hours of careful work.
- **Other notes:** If you are coming in a group or during Geode Fest, the owner will do some "grooming" to expose new material.

## (Gary) Jacobs Geode Shop and Mine

823 E County Rd 1220, Hamilton, IL; 217-847-3509

- **Difficulty level:** Easy to medium. There are many geodes that can be harvested from exposed areas within this large geode mine. Many geodes have broken loose and are easily found along the bottom rims of the exposed rock-and-clay walls. There are alluvial dirt-and-rock walls, as well, that yield plentiful geodes, both small and large. Finally, there is a stream that runs through the property that is great for finding weathered-out geodes.

- **Accessibility:** Parking area is at the mine site, so there is no significant walking.

- **Quantity, variety, size:** Many smaller geodes in the 1"–3" size range with a wide range of crystal and mineral formations, and also some larger geodes

- **Other notes:** No appointment needed during the regular season of April–October. The mine is periodically groomed to expose new material.

## Dennis Stevenson Geodes

625 South 18th St, Hamilton, IL; 309-337-3089

- **Difficulty level:** Medium to easy. Most of the hunting is done in a creek bed that has clay embankments, where you can dig out layers of clay with shovels and pickaxes to expose new material. After heavy rains, you can find many geodes on the gravel bars along the streambed or in the water itself. There is also some hillside and berm hunting.

- **Accessibility:** Moderate, as you'll need to be able and willing to walk in the streambed which is rocky and uneven, but if you pace yourself and hunt mostly on the gravel bars, it can be easy.

- **Quantity, variety, size:** Good variety of geode types and sizes

- **Other notes:** Individuals and groups are welcome.

## Nick's Geodes

251 North 7th Street, Hamilton, IL; 217-219-1263

- **Difficulty level:** Medium to easy. All of the hunting is done in a creek bed that has clay embankments, where you can dig out layers of clay with shovels and pickaxes to expose new material. After heavy rains, you can find many geodes on the gravel bars along the streambed or in the water itself.

- **Accessibility:** Moderate, as you'll need to be able and willing to walk in the streambed which is rocky and uneven, but if you pace yourself and hunt mostly on the gravel bars, it can be easy.

- **Quantity, variety, size:** Average sizes are 2"–4", but several larger geodes of 8"–10" diameter have also been found.

- **Other notes:** Individuals and groups are welcome.

## (Tim) Sheffler Rock Shop and Geode Mine

26880 Topanga Canyon Blvd, Alexandria, MO; 319-795-5013

www.facebook.com/shefflerrockshop

- **Difficulty level:** Medium to difficult. Hard rock picking and chiseling on rock walls or at ground level, which entails crouching and bending and some trench shoveling to expose geode-bearing rock.
- **Accessibility:** Easy access with just a short walk to the hunting sites. To work the rock walls, you'll have a bit more effort to ensure good footing as you work with picks and chisels.
- **Quantity, variety, size:** Outstanding variety of types and sizes of geodes.
- **Other notes:** Individuals and groups are welcome. On-site rock shop with many beautiful geodes on display.

## Additional Sites

Here are some additional sites that are open during the Geode Festival and might also be open outside the festival: Barrow, Amish North, Amish South, Fox River, Cooper, Rods, Renards.

## OTHER COLLECTING SITES

There are plentiful noncommercial collecting sites to be found, on private and public property. If hunting on private land, be sure to gain proper authorization; we provide some helpful suggestions for gaining permission throughout the Lake Superior Agates chapter. The most notable venues to be considered are rivers and streams, such as the Fox River. A canoe or kayak will help you get to places that others have difficulty accessing, which therefore tend to be more productive.

Additionally, there are farm fields with abundant rock at the surface level. As long as you're in the general range shown on the maps, you're almost certain to find some geodes in these fields. A quick scan of a local field showed some promising rocks—and a geode that had already been broken open by farm equipment.

Lastly, there are road cuts and road construction zones. While these can be incredibly productive, they can also be dangerous, and they are usually restricted by local ordinances. Check with local authorities before hunting in these sites!

# TOOLS AND EQUIPMENT FOR GEODE EXTRACTION

Most of the equipment used for hunting and opening geodes is relatively inexpensive, and you may already own some of this equipment, especially if you rockhound for other kinds of gems and minerals. The notable exception is pipe cutting tools for opening large geodes, which can be expensive.

## General Tools and Equipment

- First aid kit
- 5-gallon pails (1–3)
- Heavy-duty pack to carry your tools
- Tool belt (optional)
- Garden shovel and hand trowel
- Drinking water and nourishing snack foods
- Insect repellent
- Sunscreen
- Sun visor or hat
- Heavy-duty work gloves and boots
- Tall rubber boots if you'll be crossing or hunting in water
- Packing material such as newspaper or brown packing paper to wrap any broken-open geodes for transport

## Specialty Tools and Equipment

Note: We recommend labeling your tools in some way to keep track of them, since there will often be many people at the site using identical tools.

- **Rock hammer pick:** by Estwing ($30)
- **Chisel of medium width and thickness (flathead screwdrivers can also be used):** by Estwing ($25)
- **Mini sledgehammer:** by Estwing ($35)
- **Paleo Pick:** by Estwing ($70)
- **Gad Pry Bar:** by Estwing ($40). Can be driven into rock and then moved back and forth to loosen chunks of limestone.
- **Knee and wrist protectors:** For hunting close to the ground ($25).
- **Face shield (or safety glasses/goggles):** Also suggest wearing long pants and shirt sleeves to protect against flying rock shards ($25).
- **Earplugs:** You can get a pack of 50 foam earplugs for about $10.

# THE KEOKUK GEODE FEST

If you have never hunted or collected Keokuk geodes, or you've hunted them but haven't had much luck finding good-quality specimens, make a date on your calendar to attend the annual Keokuk Geode Fest! Even if you've hunted geodes quite successfully, you owe it to yourself to attend this wonderful event. You'll meet people who are happy to share their knowledge, you'll see premium "show specimens" of every variety, and you'll have access to all of the collecting sites we've included in this book—and some that are only open during the festival. There are also many hands-on demonstrations, especially about opening geodes. It's a world-class rock show, and you will meet Keokuk geode enthusiasts and collectors from around the globe!

# REFERENCES AND RESOURCES

## Books

- Culp, Brad Lee and June Culp Zeitner. *Geodes: Natures Treasures.* Gem Guides Book Co., 2006. (Well-researched and well-written book, focused on geology and differentiation of mineral inclusions within Keokuk geodes. Chapter 8 (Wonderful Warsaw) is all about Keokuk/Warsaw geodes.)

- Sinotte, Stephen R. *The Fabulous Keokuk Geodes, Vol. 1.* Wallace-Homestead Company, 1969. (Definitive book on Keokuk geode formation and types. No longer in print.)

## Periodicals

- *Rock & Gem Magazine* has numerous good articles about Warsaw-Keokuk Geodes. Here is a good recent article.

  www.rockngem.com/a-formation-without-explanation-pseudocubic-
  quartz-and-keokuk-geodes/

## Keokuk Geode Fest and Keokuk Area Convention & Tourism Bureau

- 319-524-5599; www.keokukiowatourism.org

## Rock Clubs

- Cedar Valley Rocks & Minerals Society, Cedar Rapids, IA
  www.cedarvalleyrockclub.org

## Websites and Reference Information

- www.geodegallery.com/keokuk.html
- rockhoundbill.blogspot.com/2015/04/march2015geodes.html
- scholarworks.uni.edu/cgi/viewcontent.cgi?article=2300&context=pias

# FAIRBURN, TEEPEE CANYON, SCENIC BLACK, BUBBLEGUM, AND PRAIRIE AGATES

Western South Dakota is truly blessed with agates that are incredibly beautiful and diverse. They can also be quite valuable, with the most sought-after being the Fairburn agate. Fairburn hunting can even rival gold prospecting in terms of value obtained per time spent hunting. But Fairburn agates are exceedingly rare, and it takes significant effort, patience, and even a good bit of luck to find good-quality specimens. Next in effort and value are Teepee Canyon agates. These brilliantly colored agates occur in a small area near the town of Custer, and they can be found more readily than Fairburns, but that can involve climbing steep hillsides and digging or breaking them out with trenching shovels, chisels, and hammers. Next in the lineup are Scenic black agates, an often overlooked but reasonably abundant variety that offers strikingly beautiful colors and patterns. Coming in number four is the bubblegum agate, the exterior of which resembles chewed gum (especially those that are pink in color), but they often have beautiful patterns and bright and colorful insides when cut open. And finally, there is the lowly prairie agate, which, while quite varied and beautiful across a range of color schemes, is so abundant that many agate hunters in western South Dakota scoff at anyone that collects them.

Perhaps the best things about all western South Dakota agate varieties is that they can be hunted for and collected across wide ranges of publicly owned lands, without any special permit or permission needed. But still, it's critical that you obtain current information and mapping concerning the land you'll be on and who owns it. It's also important to stay up-to-date on any new rules and regulations pertaining to collecting and what kinds of vehicles (ATVs, trucks, etc.) are permitted in different areas. You will often be hunting and

collecting in remote areas, so your choice of vehicles is important and a subject of safety, given both the rugged terrain and the threat of weather turning the ground to mud. Also make note that even in areas marked as public land on BLM (Bureau of Land Management) maps, there may be some private and commercial properties that are bounded by fences. You must obtain direct permission from the owners and operators of these properties before hunting and collecting, and you must obey all signs prohibiting entry.

You'll be sure to find many other "treasures" when hunting for agates in western South Dakota. Take careful note that **the Forest Service strictly prohibits collecting certain things, such as historical artifacts, vertebrate fossils, and petrified wood.** We provide more information about this later in the chapter.

## FAIRBURN AGATES

Fairburn agates were first discovered in significant volume close to the tiny town of Fairburn, South Dakota. Wile exceedingly rare, they can be found across a wide expanse in southwestern South Dakota and into northern Nebraska.

Fairburn agates are a type of fortification agate—they have concentric patterns or rings. Fairburns, sometimes called "burns" for short, come in a dazzling array of colors, but their pattern styles are remarkably consistent and generally referred to as a "holly leaf" because of their crisply defined outlines with precise angular points.

### Fairburn Agate Types and Features

**Solids:** These highly valued agates have completely weathered out of their host stone—a jasper concretion inside of surrounding limestone. In this book, we will mostly refer to jasper as the host stone of Fairburn agates.

**Agate in host:** This next-most sought-after agate type is a high-quality agate still surrounded by its host material, which is usually a reddish brown, dark-black, or caramel-colored jasper. The actual agate appears as a kind of "seam" in the host stone, or as a "full-face" on the flip side of what looks to be a simple piece of jasper. Expert Fairburn agate hunters will tell you that

some of their best finds are "flips," found by flipping over plain jasper rocks and finding a gorgeous Fairburn agate.

**Signers:** These show "signs" of agate in the host stone, but not much more. They have a minimal Fairburn agate pattern and maybe only 1–3 fortification rings. As such, they are neither very beautiful nor valuable.

**Frog skin:** Some Fairburn agates are said to have "frog skin," which refers to a lacy and bubbly appearance on the outer husk.

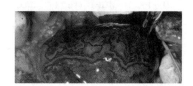

## Fairburn Agate Regional Variations

**Fairburn and Oelrichs:** Noted for the prevalence of caramel and white color variations, with some nice rose colors as well

**Railroad Buttes:** Noted for the prevalence of caramel, rose, and white color variations

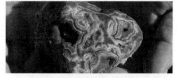

**Indian Creek:** Noted for intense blue and black color variations

**Cheyenne River:** Noted for blue and black color variations, but nearly all colors can be found, since the river carries rocks from all across the area

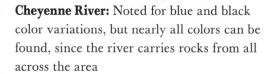

**Weta, Wasta, Conata:** Noted for intricate and lacy pattern and color variations, especially rose, peach, caramel, and white

# Imposters

These are stones that on the surface give the hint of being a Fairburn agate, labeled "teasers" by Fairburn hunters.

**Lace agates:** These aren't an official agate variety, but they do have fortification patterns. What differentiates them from Fairburns is their wavier and rounder pattern versus the tight "holly leaf" fortification rings of Fairburns. They are also milkier, and their colors are less distinctive.

**Prairie agates:** Prairies are undoubtedly the beginning Fairburn agate hunter's greatest teaser. You will fill backpacks and buckets with these beautiful stones before you finally get to the point where you've carried enough of them home to place on window ledges, in rock gardens, etc. And there are some very large pieces to be found, weighing 3 to 10 pounds! Because of the similar color schemes, often intensive banding, and "frog skin" patterns, these stones are sure to get your attention. But the pattern is rarely concentric fortification bands, and it's nowhere near as tight as Fairburn agate pattern.

**Bubblegum agates:** This relatively abundant variety of agate is actually a form of eye agate, though not all specimens have well-defined eye formations. They come in a stunning array of colors, both inside and out, and sometimes they show highly detailed pattern that can be confused with Fairburn agate pattern. Some of these are even referred to as "Fairburn bubblegums."

**Teepee Canyon agates:** Because they have the same intricate "holly leaf" fortification patterns, and sometimes share a common color scheme, they can easily be mistaken for Fairburns. But they are seldom found in the Buffalo Gap National Grassland hunting locales where Fairburns are found. The most distinguishing features that set them apart are the occurrence of deep-red surrounding matrix and the chalky tan-colored host stone that will almost always accompany Teepee Canyon agates. This variety of agates is highly prized and valued in its own right.

**Jasper:** This is the host stone for Fairburn agate formation. It comes in all of the color shades that are common with Fairburns, including the dark-brown overlays. In fact, you should train your eye to look for jasper that is showing multiple colors, such as dark brown, caramel, white, deep red, black, and deep blue as shown on these sample specimens.

## TEEPEE CANYON AGATES

Teepee Canyon agates are found in and around the Teepee Canyon area, just west of the town of Custer, South Dakota. They are rare due to the limited hunting range.

Premium specimens display a range of stunningly brilliant and beautiful colors, including burnt orange, yellow, white, pink, and purple. Lower-grade specimens have primarily the burnt orange and white patterns.

There is a significant range of colors and patterns in the Teepee Canyon agate "family." While orange, yellow, white, and purple are common, and tight fortification banding patterns are predominant, there are many other beautiful and unique pattern and color variations.

Like Scenic black agates, Teepee Canyon agates occur inside of concretions. However, they are identified not by any exterior color, but rather by the rounded or nodular shape that indicates the possibility of agate formation inside. As such, Teepee Canyon agates must also be cut or broken open to reveal the beautiful agate colors and patterns.

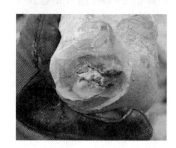

Of all the western South Dakota agates, Teepees are the only variety that involve hard rock mining with sledgehammers, wedges, pry bars, and trenching shovels to free them from host limestone formations.

As of this printing, amateur rockhounding is permitted in Teepee Canyon, though there are restrictions as to time of year, road conditions, and the amount of material that can be worked per person per day (one cubic meter).

## Imposters

Teepee Canyon agates are sometimes confused with Fairburn agates because of their intricate patterns and vibrant colors, and because weathered-out specimens can be found in some of the same hunting locales and venues as Fairburn agates.

# SCENIC BLACK AGATES

Scenic black agates are found near to the town of Scenic, South Dakota. They have a striking jet-black color that is offset by a range of bright-white, gray, and powder-blue colors and patterns.

The productive hunting range for Scenic black agates is very small and centered along Indian Creek near Scenic. Due to the small hunting range, Scenic black agates are relatively rare.

These agates appear as tan-to-gray clay concretions, with dark-black patches and protrusions that tip you off to the possibility that they are agates. They often need to be cut open to display their banding patterns.

In addition to their beautiful color schemes, Scenic black agates also have fluorescent properties when viewed under shortwave UV lights.

## Imposters

There are no stones that are readily confused with Scenic black agates.

# BUBBLEGUM AGATES

Bubblegum agates get their name from the fact that they sometimes look like a piece of chewed bubblegum, which certainly is not an appealing invitation to hunt or collect them. They are common in the western end of Buffalo Gap National Grassland.

Despite the somewhat uninviting name, both inside and out there is real beauty and appeal to these agates and they are also suitable for jewelry-making. The range of colors is too long to list, and many bubblegum agates have very bright colors, especially when cut open.

Bubblegum agates are a kind of eye agate, with eyes frequently seen on good-quality specimens.

"Bubbles," as they are sometimes called, are found in a wide hunting range that substantially overlaps with Fairburn agates, but it's primarily located at the northwestern end of the Fairburn range.

## Imposters

There are no stones that are readily confused with bubblegum agates. Some specimens with intricate banding patterns are referred to as "Fairburn bubblegums," but they are not Fairburn agates, just high-quality bubblegum agates.

# PRAIRIE AGATES

Prairie Agates are named for their occurrence across a wide expanse of prairie. They are also called "picture rock."

Prairie agates are abundant and found across the entire hunting range for Fairburn agates.

Like bubblegum agates, prairies have a reputation of being a low-grade and worthless variety of agate. However, like the bubblegums, prairie agates in fact have a wonderful variety of beautiful colors and some distinctive patterns. The most common colors are caramel and white, which is also a common color scheme for Fairburn agates.

These agates don't need to be cut open, but they can be cut and polished. If nothing else, prairie agates make for a lovely rock garden complement.

A note of caution for anyone new to rockhounding in western South Dakota is that because of their abundance and the occurrence of very large specimens weighing several pounds, one should substantially limit the number of prairie agates they collect. Periodically you can sit and cull out lower-grade specimens so that you don't become exhausted from hauling a heavy bucket or backpack.

## Imposters

There are no stones that hunters readily mistake for prairie agates, but it is common for beginning hunters to think that more-intensely patterned prairie agates are Fairburn agates. One example is darker-colored prairie agates that exhibit a "frog skin" pattern that is also found on some Fairburn agates.

# SOUTH DAKOTA AGATE PROSPECTING REGIONS

This map illustrates the rough boundaries of the various hunting venues for western South Dakota agates. There is considerable overlap in these areas, and agates can be found outside of the boundaries shown on the maps, but the areas shown provide the highest concentrations of productive hunting areas and are all publicly accessible. The Cheyenne River runs diagonally through the entire region, and, as such, it is also one of the hunting venues we cover.

**South Dakota Agate Prospecting Regions**

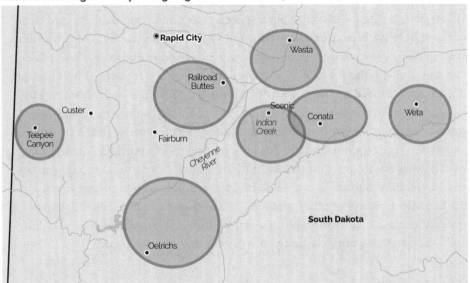

# GENERAL PROSPECTING AND HUNTING PROCESS

Because the vast majority of hunting venues reside on public lands, the prospecting process for all South Dakota agate varieties is greatly simplified. Once you know the general locale(s) where each variety can be found, it's mostly a matter of scouting those locales and determining the best ways to access areas that are often quite remote. This is especially true for Fairburn agates because, like most rare and valuable gems and minerals, any area that is readily accessible has been hunted extensively. For example, the tiny town of Fairburn (population: 85), for which Fairburn agates are named, is one of the first stops for inexperienced hunters of these prized gemstones, and to be fair, there are still nice agates being found there. We will help you hone in on the most productive areas to start your search, and we'll give you some tips on how best to access them.

As with other gems and minerals that have significant diversity, you'll need to acquaint yourself with the appearance of each type of western South Dakota agate variety, specifically how they appear in the rough. This is especially true for Fairburn agates because there are several kinds of rocks and minerals that have similar exterior textures and color schemes. As part of the learning curve, and sometimes out of sheer frustration, most newbies to Fairburn hunting will collect many prairie agates in hope that they've actually found a Fairburn. And all of the western South Dakota varieties have substantially different exterior characteristics than their beautiful inside patterns, unless of course the agate has been broken or weathered, exposing the inside color and pattern.

When prospecting for Fairburn agates, keep your mind open to all of your opportunities. Because Fairburns are so rare and valuable, they are hunted aggressively, even in remote areas. Because of this, many modern-day finds result from things like new landscaping rock being placed at commercial or residential buildings or from erosion caused by heavy rains or snowmelt. And since the Fairburn agate hunting range overlaps with bubblegum, Scenic black, and prairie agates, we combine the hunting process details for multiple agate types within each hunting venue. We recommend that instead of putting all of your effort into finding strictly Fairburn agates, you should hunt for multiple varieties at the same time, or else you may end up leaving some beauties behind. Also keep an eye out for the boundless variety of other prizes to be found, such as rose quartz, selenite crystals, tourmaline, fossils, and so much more! Plus this way, even if you don't find a Fairburn, it's unlikely that you will go home empty-handed.

## Safety Factors

There are many safety factors to be considered in the Black Hills and the grasslands of western South Dakota.

- **Remoteness:** Disorientation and getting lost are perhaps the greatest dangers. Most of the hunting venues for agates are quite remote, and you will often find yourself completely alone, possibly a substantial distance from your vehicle, and without reliable cell phone service. For this reason, we strongly recommend hunting with one or more partners in case of injury or other problems that might arise. Additionally, we advise that until you've become familiar with your hunting domains, you should use paper maps in addition to cell phones and other electronic GPS devices, which might run out of battery or lose signal strength. Staying in sight of your vehicle is another suggestion, especially since there are often few distinctive landmarks.

- **Weather:** Heat exhaustion and dehydration can occur on hot and cloudless days in the grasslands. Be sure to bring plenty of drinking water, and manage your supply so that you don't run out before getting back to civilization. Bring enough fluids so that some is left in your vehicle.

- **Roads:** Weather and "gumbo mud" are two related safety factors. Again, because you will often be hunting in remote areas that might only be accessible by dirt or gravel roads, check the weather forecast before heading out. If there is a chance of significant rainfall, you should cancel your plans! With rain, the heavy clay soil in the grasslands turns into a thick gumbo mud that **even good 4x4 vehicles cannot get through!**

- **Rattlesnakes:** Prairie rattlesnakes are venomous, and while they are somewhat rare, most experienced agate hunters in western South Dakota have had at least one encounter. The best advice is to look closely before you bend and reach to pick up something with a colorful and distinctive pattern, especially if it's surrounded by grass or weeds. Get in the habit of looking twice to validate that it's not alive! Note that there are other nonvenomous snakes that you might confuse with rattlers, such as bull snakes, which have similar markings to the untrained eye, and they are usually larger than prairie rattlers. Regardless, you are best to keep your distance from all snakes!

- **Mountain lions:** These big cats are a rare sighting in western South Dakota. They tend to shy away from human contact, but it's one more reason to be aware of your surroundings. If you do spot a mountain lion, don't run, as this might startle it and send it into attack mode. Stay as calm as possible, and either hold your ground or back away slowly. Never walk towards the animal, as it might have young that it is tending to.

- **Cacti:** There are plenty of cacti in parts of this area, and some of them are able to penetrate the soles of your shoes. Look before you grab for a colorful rock, and check around before you sit.

### Teepee Canyon Agate Hunting Comes with Additional Precautions

- Watch out for falling rocks when working along steep rock walls or on hillsides with loose boulders. There are so many good hunting spots in the Teepee Canyon area that we generally advise against working steep rock walls.

- In some areas, you'll be climbing on steep hillsides with sharp rocks while carrying a heavy load. Take your time and choose your steps carefully, making sure you are balanced before taking another step.

- Because you'll be breaking rock chunks to find agate nodules, you must wear safety glasses or goggles and possibly a face shield to protect against sharp rock chips hitting your eyes and face.

## BUFFALO GAP NATIONAL GRASSLAND: NEAR FAIRBURN, OELRICHS, CONATA, WETA, AND WASTA

The Buffalo Gap National Grassland covers more than 900 square miles of (mostly) public land available for exploration and recreational rockhounding. It is a literal treasure trove of agates, rocks and minerals, and fossils. You don't need to obtain approval to hunt any land designated as U.S. Forest Service public land within the Grassland. Consult the Buffalo Gap National Grassland Rockhound Guide from the U.S. Forest Service, found at the link below, for current rules and restrictions concerning collecting.

www.fs.usda.gov/Internet/FSE_DOCUMENTS/fseprd584624.pdf

Any fenced or posted lands within the Grassland should be considered private property, and you must find the owners and obtain their approval to hunt or collect on those properties. Because there is such a vast amount of public productive hunting territory, it generally isn't worth the effort to obtain approval to hunt on private lands. Note that fencing along the public roadways (including unpaved roads) is not an indication of private property; this fencing is to reduce the amount of wildlife crossing the road.

## Off Highway Vehicle (OHV) Restrictions

While OHV use is allowed within much of the Grassland, you generally must stay on existing trails and roads, which sometimes are just dirt or gravel. To be sure your use of OHVs/ATVs is legal, obtain the free map and accompanying information at the links below and study it ahead of time.

www.avenzamaps.com/maps/904096buffalo-gap-national-grassland-
  wall-ranger-district-mvum

www.fs.usda.gov/detail/nebraska/home/?cid=stelprdb5097502

## Finding Good Rock Beds in the Grassland

The maps in this chapter provide target zones for good rock beds, which are extensive areas of exposed and weathered rocks. Remember that easily accessible rock beds will have seen the most hunting, so be prepared to hike or have an ATV to get farther afield to more-productive grounds. But even well-hunted areas can be productive if recently eroded by heavy rainfall or snowmelt. Here is an outline for prospecting in the Grassland.

- Decide on the types of agates you will be hunting and the venue(s) that provides the highest concentration of the varieties you are most interested in. Because there is a substantial overlap of land with all four agate varieties, you need to choose one of the varieties as your primary focus. Of course, you have the chance of finding the other varieties as well, especially prairie agates. However, if you are intent on finding Fairburn agates, you must narrow your focus and learn to mentally screen out things like prairie agates, which will distract you and become a heavy burden in your collecting pack.

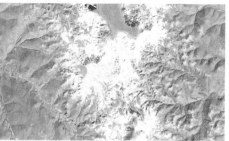

Railroad Buttes rock beds just south of Farmingdale
*Map services and data available from USGS, Nat. Geospatial Program*

- Use satellite imagery and detailed area maps, such as the U.S. Forest Service free map of the Buffalo Gap National Grassland, to familiarize yourself with the terrain and the roads of your selected target zone. Also use satellite imagery to look for large eroded areas that appear lighter colored (almost white) and that might display "alluvial fan" configurations, indicating water erosion.

- Identify roads that get you as close as possible to the areas you want to inspect.

- If you have an OHV/ATV, check the U.S. Forest Service guidelines (see page 180) to determine whether you'll be able to drive the vehicle in or near the areas you'll be prospecting.

- Plan your total trip time, and add some cushion, since the area will be new to you, and you want to have time for recording your route, coordinates, prospecting results, etc. Remember to bring plenty of snacks and water, so you don't have to cut your trip short.

## The Hunting Experience

Hunting for agates in the Buffalo Gap National Grassland is one of the most relaxing and enjoyable gemstone hunting experiences in the world! It is a vast area of public land, so you can be comfortable in the fact that you are allowed to hunt and collect. Additionally, you're in a beautiful landscape with many unique and colorful rocks and minerals weathered out, and you're often hunting in sunny weather. And lastly, you'll get plenty of exercise that generally isn't too strenuous.

**Fairburn agate:** Note the color transitions from caramel to white to rose.

**Bubblegum agate:** Note the "bubbly" exterior texture and round shape.

**Fairburn agate:** Note the pattern of concentric fortification rings.

**Fairburn agate:** Note the barely visible pattern on the "flip sides."

**Prairie agate:** Note the wavy pattern, not the finely detailed concentric fortifications of Fairburns.

## Tips for Successful Hunting

- Think small, very small: Other than prairie agates, the agates you'll be hunting for in the Grassland are 1"–4" in diameter, the features or "feature clues" that you are looking for are very fine, and you are usually looking amidst a high concentration of rocks with similar colors. You must be patient and perhaps even meticulous as you visually process hundreds and thousands of rocks.

- You must be able and willing to position yourself as close as possible to the rocks you are looking at—crouching, bending over, sitting, etc. In fact, we recommend getting an inexpensive pair of both hand and knee protectors so that you can crawl comfortably. **One thing is certain, if you are always fully upright and covering a lot of ground quickly, your chances of finding agates are very low.**

- Pick up anything that has "signature" features of the kinds of agates you are looking for—you'll probably need to pick up 10–20 stones for every one that turns out to be a Fairburn. Use your 5–10x magnifier to inspect fine details, especially when you are learning the ropes.

- When hunting in the wide-open grasslands, you will earn well-deserved breaks. Use these breaks to your advantage by finding a densely populated rock bed, pulling out your portable seat cushion, water, and snack. Now it's time to play the "flip game." This simply means identifying host jasper pieces and flipping them over to see if there is an agate showing through on the "flip side." Many world-class Fairburns have been found using this method.

- Study erosional features and patterns; areas with visible signs of erosion indicate a greater chance of renewal and turnover of rocks.

- The amount of ground you cover when in hunting mode is inversely proportional to your chances of success, especially for Fairburn agates.

- Shade is your friend, because it allows you to see more-subtle color variations and pattern details than in harsh sunlight.

- Night hunting is sometimes a great way to narrow your focus. When hunting in a rock bed, there are thousands of rocks to be scanned, and this can create visual "noise." Hunting with a flashlight greatly narrows the number of stones in your field of vision. For safety, hunt with one or more companions, and be extra alert for nocturnal wildlife.

# CHEYENNE RIVER

One of the less traveled paths for agate hunting in western South Dakota is the Cheyenne River. Public access points are limited in number, but a kayak or canoe will enable you to cover a lot of the river. And natural erosion events, such as rain, snowmelt, and flooding, result in a significant turnover of rocks. These factors make the Cheyenne River a great hunting venue for Fairburn agates.

## Finding Good Rock Hunting Areas Along the Cheyenne River

- Some recommended access points are:

    a. Where the river crosses Highway 44 just east of Creston

    b. Where the river crosses Highway 40 east of Hermosa, near Red Shirt

    c. South of Wasta, along Base Line Road

- Check with local Forest Service resources for river conditions.

- If you are going to be canoeing or kayaking, plan your trip duration based on river conditions, your skill level, and the amount of time you plan to spend hunting and collecting. Use satellite imagery to scout out sand and gravel bars for possible hunting spots and to plan where you might turn around to head back to your vehicle (unless you plan to have someone pick you up at the end of your journey).

## Land Use Restrictions

- **No hunting is allowed on the south side of the section of the river that borders the Pine Ridge Indian Reservation.**

- Badlands National Park is off-limits for hunting and collecting.

- Keep out of and away from commercial sand and gravel pits, even if they appear inactive.

- Some ranchers will tell you that you can't hunt sand and gravel bars in areas where their cows are grazing, but you can always hunt from the shoreline up to the high-water mark or embankment; but since there will be so many hunting spots along the way, you are best to just move along if they challenge you.

## The Hunting Experience

Hunting for agates along rivers and creek beds (wet or dry) comes with similar recommendations to hunting rock beds, such as: think small, get low, find less-hunted areas, look closely for snakes, and use the "flip method."

### Tips for Successful Hunting on Rivers and Streams

- Hunting closer to the water is best, because those stones have usually been deposited or turned over most recently.

- If there are feeder streams, take the time to work these as well, provided they are within allowed public lands; in general you might work them back away from the river about 100 yards.

- If there has been recent heavy rain and flooding, your chances are greatly improved even near easy-access points. But if the water is still high, make sure the river conditions are safe for your level of skill and confidence.

- Use a paddle to splash water onto rocks onshore. You'll often find that the rocks along rivers and creeks have wavy white sediment lines that are easily confused with agate banding. Getting the stones wet eliminates these lines and makes other patterns more visible. Working in teams is best, with one person splashing the rocks and one or more people inspecting them as you work down the river shores.

# INDIAN CREEK

In addition to being one of the most beautiful and panoramic hunting venues for western South Dakota agates, Indian Creek is also home to the greatest concentration of Scenic black agates, which are found almost exclusively at this location. Additionally, all of the other agate types here feature dark-black and deep-blue colors that resulted from volcanic activity and sedimentation after the agates had weathered out of their host formations. There are plentiful hunting spots across the basin, and periodic rain and snow-melt events provide regular turnover of surface stones.

## Finding Good Rock Hunting Areas at Indian Creek

In order to access the Indian Creek basin and navigate across the creek as it winds along the bottom of the basin, you must have a 4x4 vehicle with ground clearance of at least 9 inches, with 10+ inches being advisable, because you'll be traversing steep and deeply rutted creek embankments.

### Directions to Indian Creek Basin from Rapid City, SD

- Take Highway 44 east out of Rapid City about 30 miles to Creston (unincorporated).

- Continue east for about 6 miles (you'll cross the Cheyenne River).

- Turn right on Spring Draw Road going south, and drive about 5 miles until the road comes to a T at Indian Creek Road. (If you missed Spring Draw Road while on 44 and get to the town of Scenic, you can turn right on Indian Creek Road, traveling west.)

- Turn right on Indian Creek Road, going west, and travel about 3 miles to the Indian Creek Overlook, and then drive down into the Indian Creek basin on a **very steep and winding road covered with large rocks**.

- Once you get down into the basin, stay left at the fork in the gravel road. You will be traversing and crossing the Indian Creek multiple times. **You are required to keep all vehicles on existing roads**. You can stop at any one of the creek crossings and begin hunting along the creek bed and its gravel bars.

**Roads Leading to Indian Creek**

It's best to go online and print out detailed maps from this area and mark them with your planned route ahead of time. Remember that you'll be traveling on low-maintenance gravel roads.
*Map services and data available from USGS, Nat. Geospatial Program*

**Indian Creek and Surrounding Landscape**

The white-shaded areas are exposed rock beds.
*Map services and data available from USGS, Nat. Geospatial Program*

# The Hunting Experience

Hunting at Indian Creek is similar to hunting along the Cheyenne River, except that you'll be able to access much more of the available terrain, either on foot or with your 4x4 vehicle. Typically, you'll stop at one of the creek crossings and work that area up and down the creek bed at least 50 yards in each direction. Remember that the farther you walk from your vehicle, the better your chances of looking at rocks that haven't been previously hunted. And if you're up for a bit of a hike (about half a mile), there are steep hillsides with rock beds at the base to the south and north of the Indian Creek Basin. Because the hillsides are steep, there is a lot of ongoing erosion and exposure of new material. Additional hunting tips for Indian Creek include:

- All of the agate types other than Scenic black agates found at Indian Creek are coated with a dark-black material, which resulted from volcanic activity and sedimentation. In addition to the exterior coating, most of the agates have either dark-black or deep-blue color schemes. This makes Fairburn agates especially beautiful, but they're more difficult to spot, except when there is a bright-white or rose offsetting color.

- Bubblegum and prairie agates will show much more striking patterns, which is good. However, that makes them easier to confuse with Fairburns.

- Scenic black agates are one of the lesser known varieties of western South Dakota agates, despite the fact that some have intensely beautiful dark-black and bright-white patterns, deep-blue colors, and botryoidal crystals. In addition, they are fluorescent when viewed under shortwave UV light. These agates will be easier to find than Fairburns, because they are less sought-after and because their exterior color scheme is so unique, featuring a tan-colored exterior with dark-black protrusions and inclusions. Although many of the Scenic black agates are quite plain on the outside, they quite frequently have distinctive interior patterns, which means you'll need a rock saw to discover and enjoy their inner beauty.

Scenic black agate

Bubblegum agate with black exterior and exposed white geode center

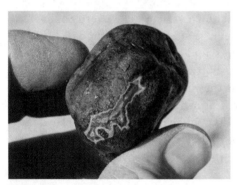

Fairburn with beautiful black and blue colors

Black jasper—a Fairburn "signer"

Prairie agates with distinctive black and white colors

# URBAN PROSPECTING: LANDSCAPING AND ROOFING ROCK

A nice variety of fresh gravel!

You might wonder whether this venue and method of hunting for agates is worthwhile. It is! Accessing commercial gravel mining operations is quite difficult, but the freshly mined and washed rock they produce can be found after it has left the mining sites. Landscaping and roofing rock often yields premium agates, but you must ask permission from the property owners before hunting. Of course, being a patron of a given restaurant or retail store goes a long way toward getting permission. Urban prospecting also allows direct vehicle access, limiting the physical exertion required.

## Finding Good Landscaping Rock

Finding promising landscaping and roofing rock is done through a process called "urban prospecting." Agate hunters who focus on this method learn how to keep track of new construction that might use fresh rock for landscaping or roofing, which offers a greater probability of finding quality agates than rock that has been searched many times.

Some information can be obtained from publicly available construction permits, but the best bet is simply to drive around and look for construction sites and then drive by periodically to follow the progress. You can learn if and when they'll be using rock, either for roofing or landscaping, by having a quick chat with the construction workers. And bringing a dozen donuts to the work crew might just help your chances of being the first on scene after a large dump truck of fresh rock shows up!

Another great way to access landscaping gravel is by visiting residential landscaping businesses, which often have large piles of rock of different sizes. If you are a customer of a local landscaping business, you might have better luck getting approval to periodically stop by and hunt for agates.

Don't completely give up on hunting at established buildings (commercial or residential), however. The rock may never have been thoroughly searched by an experienced agate hunter, or it might have recently been turned over. Many great agates have been found at long-established locations.

## Obtaining Approval to Hunt and Collect

When seeking approval, always make sure to properly introduce yourself and ask about any restrictions they have, such as where or when you can hunt. At new construction sites, it's best to talk to the crew foreman, and at established buildings or landscaping businesses, seek out the owner or manager.

## The Hunting Experience

Landscaping and roofing rock provides a large volume of cleaned and sorted rock—truly an agate hunters dream come true! We offer the following tips:

- Patience goes a long way—with so much rock available to look at, it's easy to lose focus and move too quickly. Stand in one place for 10 to 30 seconds at a time, carefully surveying the rock within a given "vision frame" (such as a 7x7-foot square), and then move to the next "vision frame." If you are hunting on all fours, it will naturally slow your movement.

- Ask if you can climb on any rock piles and move rock around. If so, thoroughly inspect the top layer of rock first.

- If the rock is already spread, make sure to not only inspect the top layer of rock, but to also look through and beneath the top layer. You can use your feet to gently move and turn over the top layer of rock, but be sure that you always leave things well-groomed and looking nice.

Fine Fairburn agate detail hiding just beneath the top layer of rock

A quintessential South Dakota bubblegum agate—luckily, they don't stick to your shoes!

A beautiful and well-defined black-and-blue prairie agate

Scenic black agate

# GRAVEL PITS

It's nearly impossible to gain access to a commercial gravel mining operation in western South Dakota. Some of the county owned and operated pits might provide a better opportunity to gain access. Consult the Lake Superior Agates chapter for the general processes of obtaining permission and hunting within gravel pits. Additionally, we provide the following references for locating and initiating contact with gravel pits in the Grassland and along the Cheyenne River:

- Use satellite imagery to search for active gravel pits, such as this example of the Wasta gravel pit below.

*Map services and data available from USGS, Nat. Geospatial Program*

- South Dakota provides a lookup database for gravel mining operations (see the link below). Start by entering: Rapid City, SD, USA. After this you can zoom in or out on the screen, and you'll be presented with a view of active (red dot) and inactive (green dot) sand and gravel pits. You can check these against satellite imagery to judge whether the operations are current as of the last satellite photo updates. If you find a good match, then you might visit the site to initiate contact; follow the guidelines and instructions in the Lake Superior Agates chapter gravel pit section (page 28).

  sdbit.maps.arcgis.com/apps/webappviewer/indexhtml?id=4046cfb6c4c240
      87831e18c6255466ae

## TEEPEE CANYON

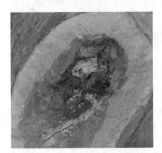

Teepee Canyon agate prospecting and hunting is something of a "last frontier" for agate hunting in western South Dakota. While it can be a physically demanding pursuit, there is a considerable amount of "low hanging fruit" in terms of high-quality agates to be found. Many magazine articles have been written about laborious trench digging on sweltering hot days. But in reality, you might not have to do any excavation at all. And you can plan to work at times of the year when temperatures are moderate, or even a bit cold. A cloudy day of 50–70 degrees works great. While you can climb steep rock hillsides to get to some dig sites, there are also scrap piles on flatter ground that have chunks of limestone containing

Teepee Canyon agate nodules; a bit of hammer and chisel activity will break them free. And you'll probably find some excellent broken agate pieces that have been discarded by "trophy" agate hunters; these are excellent for lapidary work.

So why consider Teepee Canyon agates at all when there are so many other agates to be found in easier and less remote hunting venues? To start with, your chance of success is higher, especially compared to Fairburns. And these "cousins" of Fairburn agates have a range of stunningly beautiful colors and patterns. Finally, you'll enjoy a magnificently scenic drive all the way from Rapid City to Teepee Canyon. It's something of a different world, one that many rockhounding enthusiasts deeply respect and treasure.

## Finding Teepee Canyon and Good Hunting Spots

### Directions to Teepee Canyon from Custer, SD

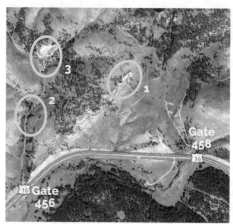

Map services and data available from USGS, Nat. Geospatial Program

- Travel west from Custer on US-16 about 12 miles to the Jewel Cave Visitor Center entrance, and then continue west another 4 miles, passing Mud Springs Road on the right and then Mann Road on the left before turning onto a gated but unnamed road on the right/ north side of the road at **Marker #458**. Then bear left at the fork, and left again at the second fork. You'll be able to spot tailing piles of whitish-colored limestone (location 1 on the map).

- You can travel another mile to a second entrance on the north side of US-16 at **Marker #456**. A short distance in on the left you'll spot some tailing piles up the hillside (location #2 on map), or you can drive farther in and spot another larger section of tailing piles on the right (location #3).

## Obtaining Approval to Hunt and Collect

Because Teepee Canyon is within U.S. Forest Service lands, you don't need to ask permission to dig for and collect agates. However, if you are digging out new material, you are restricted to no more than 1 cubic meter per person per day. There can also be access restrictions caused by poor condition of the dirt access roads. To get current information, contact the Black Hills National Forest Supervisor's Office/Hell Canyon Ranger District at 605-673-9200.

There is no restriction on hunting through the vast amounts of loose material lying around. Many people that aren't up for the hard rock mining required to extract Teepee Canyon agate nodules choose to carefully inspect the loose rocks, and many report coming away with nice specimens, even if they are only partial.

## The Hunting Experience

The three hunting options at Teepee Canyon described here are listed in order of relative ease, considering accessibility, work effort, and risk. First is working the waste piles, second is trenching and digging out new material, and third is working rock walls to break out limestone chunks and agate nodules. The second method offers the chance of better quality and larger agate nodules. The third option also provides opportunities, but it comes with a warning of the substantial risk of personal injury—and one might easily be tempted to go after large visible nodules. For each of the hunting methods, it's valuable to know whether you are hunting in material that might yield Teepee Canyon agates. If you see clues to finding and identifying Teepees, then you know that agate nodules are likely nearby. The most notable clues are:

| | | |
|---|---|---|
| Shell fossil imprints | Deep-orange chalcedony matrix | Rounded bulges in chunks of limestone |

- Waste rock heaps are large and abundant within Teepee Canyon. It can truly be said that "One man's trash is another man's treasure!" when you are hunting for agates in these piles of broken rock, as seen in the first photo on page 198. Scouting among the rock might yield an agate nodule (or a portion thereof) just lying there for the taking, as in the second photo. Plus look for the telltale rounded bulges of an agate nodule, such as in the third photo. You can also break open larger chunks of rock in hopes of exposing nodules inside the rock, such as in the fourth image, which shows a nondescript agate nodule.

- Trenching and digging entails significant labor and usually climbing steep, rocky hillsides to get to places where you can dig out new material. Plan ahead and wear sturdy hiking boots (possibly steel-toed), and bring plenty of water and healthy snacks. Work with a plan, so you don't need to climb up and down the hillsides more than necessary. It's helpful to work where there has already been some digging. You won't have to break new ground, and right away you can bring out material that has agate nodules. As you bring out new material, set it aside until you can do further work to extract and open nodules. You might dig out a quarter or a half of your daily limit, and then take a break to do the extraction and opening. Always use caution when digging deep into a hillside to make sure that large rock chunks don't fall onto your head or body. And be aware that snakes sometimes seek shelter from the elements in existing dig sites!

- **Hunting in limestone rock faces and overburden comes with high risk.** While trophy nodules can be found, the risk and corresponding effort to extract them without injury is so high that we generally discourage people from even trying.

# Extracting and Opening Nodules

Chisels and hammers are used for extracting nodules and breaking them open at the collection site, which you might want to do to limit the load you need to carry, especially if traversing steep and rocky hillsides. You might, however, choose to wait until you get home to extract any nodules from the host rock, since breaking them free with a chisel and hammer comes with the risk of fracturing the agate; at home, you might have the option to saw your nodules open. That being said, if there are existing fracture lines on the nodules that you have extracted, you're generally safe to apply the chisel along that line and tap gently until they break open.

This somewhat flat nodule was able to be freed from the limestone block with just a bit of light tapping, with the chisel about ⅛" from the nodule itself. A barely visible hairline fracture suggested it could be broken open with the chisel rather than bringing it back to the workshop for sawing. The inside showed almost no pattern, so this nodule was left at the site and didn't have to be carted down the steep hillside in the collecting pack.

This one showed as a small rounded bulge on the face of a big limestone block. Because there was already a bit of fracturing visible on the rock chunk, the chisel was used first to remove excess material. Then some light hammer tapping away from the nodule caused it to loosen up sufficiently to be removed by hand. Unfortunately, the nodule already had an inherent fracture, so it came apart in hand, but it can be cleaned up nicely with a little lapidary work.

The inside of this nodule had already been exposed on the face of a large chunk of limestone. Since there was a large break, or cleavage line, the chisel was applied along that line, and with a few moderate taps with the hammer, the limestone chunk broke and the agate nodule popped right out! This nodule has a gorgeous blue-and-white pattern.

## TOOLS AND EQUIPMENT

### General Tools and Equipment

- Sturdy and comfortable hiking boots
- Collecting pack
- First aid kit
- Food and water
- Sunscreen
- Bug repellent
- GPS unit or app for your phone
- Compass
- Binoculars
- Something soft to sit on (maybe a portable cushion)
- Small paddle for splashing water onto rocks along shorelines
- Shovel

## SPECIALTY TOOLS AND EQUIPMENT

- **Cell phone with reliable service in western South Dakota:** This is a must, due to the possibility of getting lost in remote areas, falling, or encountering rattlesnakes.

- **Polarized sunglasses, or polarized or non-tinted prescription eyeglasses if you wear them:** Regular sunglasses tend to reduce your ability to see color variations, which is a critical identifying feature of agates. Polarized sunglasses are great for reducing glare when hunting in or near the water's edge.

- **Knee and wrist protectors:** For hunting close to the ground ($25)
- **5-10x lighted magnifier:** Carson MiniBrite is one good model. These are a must for inspection and identification ($11).
- **ATV, 4x4 vehicle, canoe, or kayak:** If you don't have your own, there are sporting goods stores in the Rapid City area that rent them by the day.
- **Face shield (or safety glasses/goggles):** For Teepee Canyon agates; also suggest wearing long pants and shirt sleeves to protect against flying rock shards ($25)
- **Rock hammer pick:** by Estwing ($30)
- **Chisel of medium width and thickness (flathead screwdrivers can also be used):** by Estwing ($25)
- **Mini sledgehammer:** by Estwing ($35)
- **Paleo pick:** by Estwing ($70)
- **Gad Pry Bar:** by Estwing ($40)

# REFERENCES AND RESOURCES

- Buffalo Gap National Grassland Rockhound Guide and Rules
  www.fs.usda.gov/Internet/FSE_DOCUMENTS/fseprd584624.pdf
- Buffalo Gap National Grassland Map
- Clark, Roger. *South Dakota's Fairburn Agate.* Silverwind Agates, 1998.
- Magnuson, James. *The Fairburn Agate of the Black Hills: 100 Unique Storied Agates.* Adventure Publications, 2012.

## Facebook Groups
- Scenic Black Agates of South Dakota
  www.facebook.com/groups/1951572735117877
- Fairburn Agate of South Dakota
  www.facebook.com/groups/419965524692291

# PETOSKEY STONES

Petoskey stones are known and loved the world over, especially in Michigan, where they are the official state stone. The beauty of these stones is in their intricate patterns, which stand out boldly, especially when wet or polished. The most-prized stones are those with darker-gray colors, not only because their greater contrast highlights the patterns, but also because they typically take a polish better. Some Petoskey stones can be quite large, weighing well over a pound, with the largest ever recorded being approximately 93 pounds. As with other gemstones, people tend to prize a larger stone with a striking pattern. A high-quality piece weighing more than a pound can easily fetch over $100!

Around 400 million years ago, much of Michigan was covered by a shallow, salty sea that was home to numerous species of *Hexagonaria* corals. That genus name derives from the six-sided structure of each small "corallite"–the fossilized skeletal structure that remains from each individual coral polyp. These fossils are now part of the layers of limestone below much of Michigan, and today they can be found across the state, in places where the bedrock is exposed and pieces have weathered free.

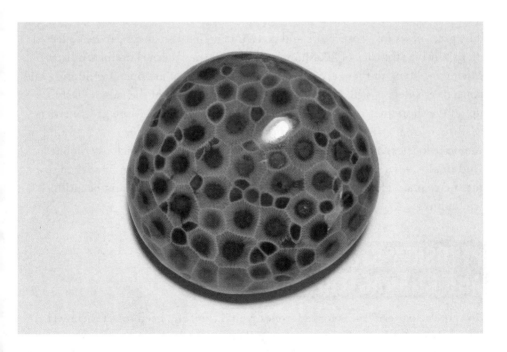

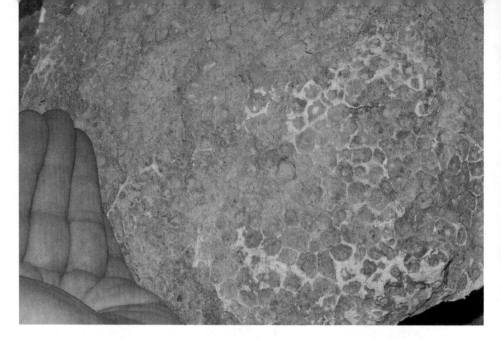

Petoskey stones originated from fossils of a specific species—*Hexagonaria percarinata*—that are most abundantly found in outcroppings of the bedrock along the northern shores of the Michigan's Lower Peninsula. After pieces of this coral weathered free, they spent thousands of years being gradually rolled smooth by the forces of the lakes, naturally tumbled by waves and sand, resulting in a beautiful smooth "finish" that is often referred to as "water-washed."

The great news for prospectors and collectors is that Petoskeys can be collected on expansive stretches of lakeshore across the far northern shorelines of Lower Michigan. Many of these areas are on public lands that are open for hunting and collecting. There is still an almost inexhaustible volume of the stones washing up on the shorelines every day, especially during high surf. More great news is that there are many other high-quality fossil types and specimens to be found in the same locales, including some rather rare types of fossils, such as trilobites. And finally, what better rock-hunting experience could a person have than one that takes place along a pristine shoreline with crashing waves and beautiful white sands.

## PETOSKEY STONE FEATURES AND CHARACTERISTICS

To spot the patterns on Petoskey stones, you'll typically need to get them wet. This is because the fossils are formed in limestone, which appears monotone when dry. Once you've gotten the stones wet, the pattern will jump out. You'll see seamlessly connected hexagonal shapes that feature intricate "septa"—fine lines that fan out to the edges from a darker center spot. This pattern is unmistakable when observed in detail. The size of these hexagonal compartments and the number of septa they contain helps differentiate one species of *Hexagonaria* from another.

Petoskey stones come with notable color variations. It has been theorized that *Hexagonaria* coral colonies were at some time infused with crude oil, and that the stones with darker colorations had a greater concentration. Darker-colored Petoskeys are more sought-after and more valuable because they tend to be more vibrant and better candidates for polishing. Another color variation that is highly prized and sought-after features the light-red to pink color hues that result from iron oxidization.

## IMPOSTERS

While the hexagonal pattern with the fine-needle fan arrays of Petoskey stones is easy to identify, there are several other kinds of beautiful, intricate, and symmetrical fossils in the same region that you might misidentify as Petoskeys, especially when smooth and wave-tumbled. The most notable of these is the Charlevoix stone, which is the fossil of a species of coral in the *Favosites* genus. Charlevoix stones don't have the finely detailed fanlike patterns of Petoskeys, and they have more-tightly packed structures that appear as columns or rows. Honeycomb coral is another prominent imposter that looks very similar to Charlevoix stones. You'll surely collect and keep these and many additional fossil treasures to display alongside your Petoskey stones!

**Charlevoix stone (*Favosites* spp.):** Charlevoix stone is the fossil type that is most frequently mistaken as a Petoskey, especially when similar to the stone in the first photo, finely tumbled and smoothed by wave action, and its coloration is very close to wave-tumbled Petoskeys.

**Honeycomb coral (*Favosites* spp.):** Honeycomb corals are beautiful, especially when they are the beautiful bleached-white color found along the lakeshores. But the coral "chambers" lack the fine details of Petoskeys.

# PETOSKEY STONE PROSPECTING REGIONS

The majority of high-quality Petoskey stones are found along the northern shores of Lower Michigan. The easternmost point of this range is Alpena on Lake Huron, and the westernmost point is Frankfort on Lake Michigan, with the namesake town of Petoskey in the middle. Petoskeys can be found all along coastal Lake Michigan and Lake Huron, but the concentration diminishes as you go farther south. Also, while Petoskeys can be found at inland locations, such as gravel pits, inland lakeshores, and along rivers and streams, the greatest concentration of quality specimens is closer to the shores of the two Great Lakes. Sections of the lakefront that are less sheltered experience more-intense wave action, and they provide the best opportunities for new stones being deposited along the shorelines.

**Petoskey Stone Prospecting Regions**

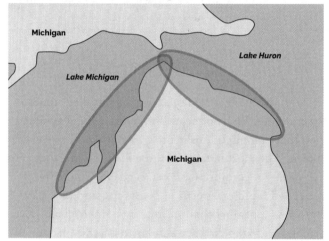

The best place to productively hunt for Petoskey stones is in Michigan state parks. There are other parks that you can hunt at as well, but you must get approval first. See the list of suggested hunting locations on the next page. Here is some basic current information on hunting and collecting at parks:

- National Parks do not allow you to take any stones out of the park.

- Michigan state parks allow hunting and collecting with the following restrictions:

  - An individual can only collect 25 pounds a year from public land.

  - Any specimen that exceeds 25 pounds must be left where it is found.

- City, county, and regional parks require checking with local park personnel before collecting. You can check county websites for contact information in the following counties: Benzie, Leelanau, Grand Traverse, Antrim, Charlevoix, Cheboygan, Presque Isle, and Alpena.

# Detailed List of Suggested Hunting Locations

The list below starts in Manistee, proceeds north and west along Lake Michigan, and then south and east along Lake Huron to Alpena.

| Location | Location Type | Venue Type |
| --- | --- | --- |
| Orchard Beach State Park | State park | Lake Michigan |
| Leelanau State Park | State park | Lake Michigan |
| Lake Leelanau | Lake in Leelanau County | Inland lake |
| Crystal Lake | Lake in Benzie County | Inland lake |
| Platte Lake | Lake in Benzie County | Inland lake |
| Empire Beach | Empire city park | Lake Michigan |
| Glen Lake | Lake in Leelanau County | Inland lake |
| Traverse City State Park | State park | Lake Michigan |
| Interlochen State Park | State park | Inland lake |
| Barnes Park | Antrim County park | Lake Michigan |
| Fisherman's Island State Park | State park | Lake Michigan |
| Michigan Beach Park | Charlevoix city park | Lake Michigan |
| North Point Nature Preserve | Charlevoix Township park | Lake Michigan |
| Torch Lake | Lake in Antrim County | Inland lake |
| Elk Lake | Lake in Antrim and Lake Traverse Counties | Inland lake |
| Lake Skegemog | Lake in Antrim, Grand Traverse, and Kalkaska Counties | Inland lake |
| Lake Charlevoix | Lake in Charlevoix County | Inland lake |
| Young State Park | State park | Inland lake |
| Petoskey State Park | State park | Lake Michigan |
| Magnus Park | Petoskey city park | Lake Michigan |
| Bayfront Park | Petoskey city park | Lake Michigan |
| Sunset Parks | Petoskey city park | Lake Michigan |
| Wilderness State Park | State park | Lake Michigan |
| Cheboygan State Park | State park | Lake Huron |
| Aloha State Park | State park | Inland lake |
| Burt Lake | Lake in Cheboygan County | Inland lake |
| Mullett Lake | Lake in Cheboygan County | Inland lake |
| Hoeft State Park | State park | Lake Huron |
| Thompson's Harbor State Park | State park | Lake Huron |
| Rockport State Recreation Area | State park | Lake Huron |
| Grand Lake | Lake in Presque Isle County | Inland lake |
| Thunder Bay River State Forest | State forest | Lake Huron |

# GENERAL PROSPECTING AND HUNTING PROCESS

The best hunting results will come after a long winter of ice sheets pushing new rock towards the shore and after big storms with heavy surf. Continuous and rolling wave action moves and refreshes the stones near shore, making such places great for hunting. And it's much easier to spot Petoskeys when they are wet, so hunting right at the shoreline allows you to splash or pour lake water onto dry stones on shore. If you are hunting in a field or gravel pit, your best option is to hunt on a rainy day.

## Safety Factors

**Waves:** The most critical safety factor regards hunting in rough surf. While these conditions bring opportunity, they also bring danger, possibly knocking you off balance and into the water. Heavy waves can push you into sharp rocks or pull you into deeper water. Given the relative abundance of Petoskey stones (compared to agates or gold, for example), there is no reason to take risks around the big lakes.

**Weather:** Overexposure to cold and damp conditions can be common along the Great Lakes. Dress appropriately, with water-repellent gear from head to toe if temperatures are less than 50 degrees.

# PROSPECTING AND HUNTING VENUES

Other than state parks, or other public venues where hunting and collecting is allowed, you must find the property owners and request their permission. The Lake Superior Agates chapter provides some helpful guidelines on how to track down landowners and some conversation starters for requesting approval.

## Lake Michigan and Lake Huron Shorelines

### Finding Good Hunting Shores

The best shoreline areas for hunting Petoskey stones have the following characteristics:

- Active surf with minimal natural or man-made "breakers," which substantially reduce wave action
- Large volume of rocks that have been "tumbled" smooth by wave action (instead of rough and broken rocks)

- Minimal signs of previous foot traffic in the rock on shore
- Less-than-easy access, such as requiring a hike or even a canoe or kayak, which reduces the number of other hunters and collectors you are competing with

Finding the areas that meet these general requirements often involves driving along roads nearest the shoreline and periodically getting out to inspect. If there are any access points marked as private or no trespassing, you must, of course, talk with the landowner before entering.

## The Hunting Experience

In general, hunting lakeshores can be a serene and even contemplative experience, but it can also be physically and mentally intensive if hunting in active surf or moving surface stones to see what lies beneath. In order of priority, we suggest the following hunting methods:

- Hunting at the water's edge is the best, especially if there is moderate wave action that is moving a lot of rocks around near the shoreline. You can either stand in the shallow water or just short of where the waves are reaching. You will be presented with a constantly changing set of rocks that are already wet, which is optimal for spotting Petoskey stone patterns. After every third or fourth wave, move laterally down the shoreline.

- Hunting rocks already on the shore is a bit more difficult. You'll have to move away the top layers with your feet or possibly a heavy metal rake, but either way, you'll need to confine this effort to small and medium-size rocks. Start near the water's edge, and either use a paddle to splash water onto the top layer of stones, or just use your foot to push away the top layer and expose a wet layer directly beneath, continually moving down the shoreline. After this you can begin looking at rocks farther from the shoreline. Fill your bucket with lake water, and splash the water onto rocks you want to inspect. It's great to use a buddy system for both the splash paddle and bucket methods, taking turns splashing and fetching the water.

- It's hard to spot patterns in deeper water, but it does provide an opportunity to find some larger Petoskeys that haven't made it onshore. We recommend wearing polarized glasses (clear or sunglasses) to minimize the surface glare on sunny days. You'll also want to have a treasure scoop tool to scoop stones off the bottom where it's too deep to reach them by hand. You can even hunt while snorkeling, or swimming with a diving mask or goggles. Make sure that you are staying in your safety zone when it comes to swimming ability and surf conditions. It's also a good idea to use the buddy system to keep an eye on each other.

**Shoreline Scenario 1:** A partially tumbled Petoskey is easier to spot when dry because it still has a rough and pitted texture, and because it retains the slightly yellower coloration found on rough stones.

**Shoreline Scenario 2:** This fully tumbled and bleached Petoskey was nearly impossible to spot when fully dry. After dipping it in the water, the coral pattern jumped out nicely.

**Shoreline Scenario 3:** This Petoskey couldn't be distinguished from all of the stones around it until we splashed some lake water onto the stones, which made the pattern emerge. After fully immersing it in water, we could see it was a high-quality specimen.

**Shoreline Scenario 4:** While walking along the shoreline in shallow and calm water, the pattern on this Petoskey was clearly visible, and it was an "easy catch."

**Shoreline Scenario 5:** There was more wave action on this part of the shoreline, so we walked a few steps, waited for the water to settle, repeated the process, and then we spotted this little beauty in the calmer water shown in the first photo.

# Gravel Bars on River Shores and Inland Lakeshores

## Finding Good Hunting Spots

Hunting for Petoskey stones along rivers and inland lakes is very similar to hunting the shores of Lakes Michigan and Huron. Look for shorelines that are "moderately accessible" (therefore less traveled and hunted) and that have an abundance of rock near the shoreline.

## The Hunting Experience

The following tips will improve your chances of success:

- Hunting close to the water is best because those stones have usually been deposited or at least turned over most recently.

- You might canoe or kayak along the shorelines to find gravel bars and beaches that cannot be easily accessed by land.

- If there has been any recent heavy rain, high surf, or higher water, your chances are greatly improved, even close to easy access points. But make sure the conditions are safe, especially along fast-moving rivers and streams.

- Use a canoe or kayak paddle to splash water onto rocks onshore to make the patterns more visible. Working in teams is best, with one person splashing the rocks and one or more people inspecting them as you work down the river shores.

## Urban Prospecting: Landscaping and Roofing Rock

Many premium Petoskey stones are found in landscaping and roofing rock. However, you must ask permission from the property owners before hunting. Being a patron of a given restaurant or other business goes a long way toward getting this permission! One other benefit of urban prospecting and hunting is the relative ease, with low physical exertion and direct vehicle access. You'll want to use a spray bottle to get the stones wet, or possibly hunt in the rain.

### Finding Good Landscaping Rock

Searching for good landscaping and roofing rock is called "urban prospecting." Rockhounds that focus on this method of hunting come to know which rocks have been thoroughly searched and which is new rock that has a greater probability of containing good Petoskeys. Keep your eyes peeled for new construction, and stop by and chat with construction workers when you see newly delivered gravel piles. Ask their permission to do a little rock hunting after hours.

Another great way to access landscaping gravel is by visiting residential landscaping businesses. These businesses often have large piles of various-size rock for sale. If you are a customer of a local landscaping business, you might have better luck getting approval to periodically stop by and hunt for Petoskey stones.

While we've focused more on finding newly delivered gravel, that doesn't mean you should ignore established buildings (commercial or residential). The rocks may never have been thoroughly searched by experienced rockhounds, or they may have recently been washed by rains or turned over and now show Petoskey features.

When seeking approval to hunt for Petoskey stones in landscape and roofing rock, always make sure to properly introduce yourself and ask about any restrictions they have, such as where or when you can hunt. At new construction sites, it's best to talk to the crew foreman, and at established buildings or landscaping businesses, seek out the owner or manager.

### The Hunting Experience

Hunting for Petoskey stones in landscaping and roofing rock means that you'll be looking at a large volume of cleaned and sorted rock. We offer the following tips:

- Hunting in a light or medium rain is your best bet, since wet Petoskeys show their pattern much better.

- If it's not raining, you need to have a good supply of water. Use a spray bottle to wet stones in a small radius around where you're standing and inspect all the wet stones, and then move to wet another batch of stones. An extra dose of patience goes a long way—because you will be looking at so much rock in one place, it's easy to lose focus and move too quickly. It's a good idea to bring along a couple of gallon jugs of tap water to refill your spray bottles.

- If the landscaping rock is in a pile, make sure that you've thoroughly inspected the top layer of rock before climbing on the pile.

- For rock that is already spread out, you can use your feet to move away the top layer and expose rocks underneath. Always be sure that you leave things well groomed so that the property owners aren't left with that chore after you've finished.

## Gravel Pits and Farm Fields

Because gravel pits have highly restricted accessibility, and because the rock in farm fields is more spread out, these two hunting venues are not recommended for beginners, especially when you consider the sheer abundance and easy accessibility in other hunting venues. The one advantage pits and fields offer is rough, natural specimens that haven't been worn smooth by wave and water tumbling. If you do desire to find and access suitable pits and farm fields, see the Lake Superior Agates chapter for more information on the process.

## TOOLS AND EQUIPMENT

### General Tools and Equipment

- Spray bottle for wetting the stones and extra water for refills
- Collecting pouch or bucket
- Small canoe or kayak paddle for splashing rocks
- Tall wading boots or sturdy water sandals
- Snorkeling gear and mask or goggles
- First aid kit

## Specialty Tools and Equipment

- **Polarized glasses (clear or sunglasses):** Standard sunglasses and progressive prescription lenses reduce color shade and faint pattern distinctions that are critical for Petoskey stone hunting.

- **Treasure scoop:** For scooping stones out of deep water ($52). https://kingsleynorth.com/treasure-scoop-42-inch.html

# REFERENCES AND RESOURCES

## Books

- Lynch, Dan R. *Petoskey Stone: Finding, Identifying, and Collecting Michigan's Most Storied Fossil.* Adventure Publications, 2019.

- Mueller, Bruce, and William H. Wilde. *The Complete Guide to Petoskey Stones.* The Petoskey Publishing Company, 2004

## Shop with Petoskey Stones

- Bailey's Place, Petoskey Stones & Stuff, Petoskey, MI www.petoskeystonesbybailey.com

- Keweenaw Gem & Gift (also known as Copper Connection), Houghton, MI copperconnection.com

## Rock Clubs

- Grand Traverse Area Rock and Mineral Club, Traverse City, MI tcrockhounds.com

## Facebook Groups

- Great Lakes Rocks and Minerals www.facebook.com/groups/106675549490547

- Michigan Rockhounds www.facebook.com/groups/MichiganFriends

# GREENSTONE AND DATOLITE

Michigan greenstone is one of the vast array of gemstones and minerals to be found along the southern shores of Lake Superior, especially on the Keweenaw Peninsula of Michigan's "UP." Also known as Isle Royale greenstone, and properly (scientifically) known as chlorastrolite, gem-quality greenstones have a stunning deep-emerald green color, and slender crystals that provide an alluring webbed appearance (sometimes referred to as a "turtleback" pattern). These stones practically glow when polished. Because of its beauty and rarity, it is the Michigan state gemstone and is prized by high-end jewelry makers. Premium-grade pieces smaller than dime-size can fetch well over $100.

Because greenstone occurs in the same range and hunting venues as Michigan copper, it is often hunted and collected by the same people that prospect for copper. It is most commonly found in old copper mine tailing piles. And while it can be collected as wave-tumbled specimens along the shores of Lake Superior, this is exceedingly rare, and in some cases prohibited, such as in Isle Royale National Park. Therefore, we will strictly focus on greenstone prospecting in abandoned copper mine sites.

This chapter will also briefly cover datolite, another rare and prized gemstone that can be found in the same hunting locations as greenstone and copper. Datolite occurs in nodular formations, and the best examples have soft and lovely colors that include yellow, orange, pink, and white, and those with web-like pattern are even more beautiful.

# GREENSTONE TYPES AND CHARACTERISTICS

Greenstone can be found in many forms, shapes, and settings, which we will refer to as "types." These photos show some of the most common.

**Hollow center:** Hollow nodules that show good pattern around the outer rim are good candidates to remove from the host stone and tumble or gently grind to expose the pattern. They are, of course, more brittle, so they'll be a good test of your hammering and chiseling skills.

**Calcite-filled:** Bright-white calcite fill can provide a stunning offset to the deep-emerald green and highlight the webbed crystals. This might be a great piece to leave in the host stone and "face polish" (see page 233).

**White and pink "eyes":** Notice the circular-shaped white inclusions. These aren't eyes but rather radial crystals, and sometimes they can be pink.

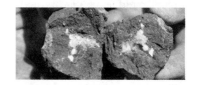

# DATOLITE TYPES AND CHARACTERISTICS

Datolite is found in the same places as copper and greenstone, so keep an eye out for it. It's good to keep a specimen handy as a visual reminder of how it appears. Datolite nodules have bubbly or botryoidal (grape-like) external surfaces that are somewhat similar to another kind of gemstone called a thunder egg. Some people refer to the exterior surface as being cauliflower-like. Datolite nodules tend to have light-gray (or purple) and chalky-white colors, as in the examples that follow. The second specimen (in the second and third photos on the next page) is a premium larger-size nodule with a striking webbed pattern on the interior.

**Rounded surface:** A nice-size datolite specimen that stands out from the broken chunks of basalt because of its more rounded and botryoidal (or bubbly) surface. Sometimes the datolite nodule will still be attached to a chunk of basalt and will need to be carefully broken free with hammer and chisel.

**Gemmy interior:** The reverse side of the nodule in the previous photo shows a gemmy interior that can be cut and polished. This is a milky-white specimen. More-prized specimens will have soft color shades, such as pink, green, yellow, or orange.

**Light-colored:** This datolite nodule stands out from the basalt chunks because of the lighter-white color and obvious rounded and botryoidal surface shape and texture. While rare, you will find specimens like this because of the constant movement of the large tailings piles.

**Web-patterned interior:** The above nodule was cut open to review this beautiful web-patterned interior, and then the interior faces were polished for display.

## IMPOSTERS

**Chlorite:** This is the primary imposter of greenstones because of its nodular form and deep-green color. Sometimes you can't tell them apart until you tumble or grind away the outer layer. If you don't find any of the fine needle fans or the "turtleback" pattern, it's probably not greenstone.

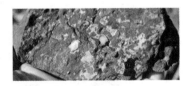

**Epidote:** Lime-green overlays on basalt and nodular inclusions have bright lime-green crystals that are much lighter in color than greenstone.

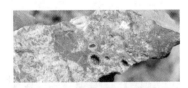

**Copper replacement agate:** Copper replacement agates have the same dark-green-coated nodular form. If you have a metal detector, you'll know it's not greenstone when you get a signal. You can also see the copper banding in copper replacement agates once you cut them open, and they don't have the trademark greenstone patterns and features.

**Prehnite:** Prehnite is often found in close proximity to greenstone, but prehnite's brighter and more translucent light-green color will make it relatively easy to distinguish from the emerald green of greenstone.

# GREENSTONE AND DATOLITE PROSPECTING REGIONS

The map below depicts known locations of where Michigan greenstone can be reliably found. These are roughly the same regions as for finding copper, except that Region 2 is considerably smaller in this case, and the most productive range within Region 1 is on the northeastern end of the Keweenaw Peninsula. Michigan greenstone can also be found, although rarely, along the north shore of Lake Superior, and on the shores of Isle Royale, as well, where collecting is prohibited.

**Greenstone and Datolite Prospecting Regions**

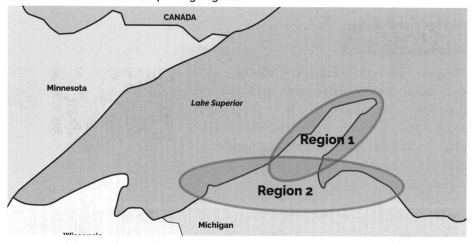

# GENERAL PROSPECTING AND HUNTING PROCESS

Here's a little-known secret and some great news for greenstone prospectors: A lot of gem-quality greenstone specimens can be found just lying on the ground at abandoned mine sites. This is probably because most people are hunting for copper and either don't know about greenstone or just don't care to collect it. If you zero in on a good spot, you'll spend the majority of your time breaking apart large basalt chunks to expose nodules and then further breaking the pieces down into smaller pieces to bring home.

As with thomsonite nodules that are still embedded in basalt chunks, the final steps of freeing the nodules from the host rock are often best done at home, where you have a stable workbench and tools that are better suited to extracting small and delicate nodules. You'll be working with tools like diamond core drilling bits, hammers and small chisels, and rotary tools.

## Safety Factors

When you're working with tools like picks and hammers, it's important to maintain a safe distance of at least 8 feet between yourself and other hunters. One swing of a pick or sledgehammer could result in traumatic injuries, either from flying rock chunks or being struck by the tool itself.

- **Safety glasses:** It's essential that you use high-quality safety glasses or goggles when working with picks and hammers. You might even consider wearing a full-face shield to protect more than just your eyes.

- **Earplugs:** Believe it or not, working around a lot of people doing pick and hammer work on hard rock can get quite loud. A simple pair of earplugs will help you avoid a pounding headache after a long day of hunting and extraction.

- **Pay attention:** When you are working on mine tailing piles with large and jagged rocks, it's important to move slowly. With each step, take your time in planting your feet to ensure that the rocks are stable enough to hold your full weight. As you begin to dig into the pile, look first before carefully tossing unwanted rocks away, and toss them safely away from any other hunters in your vicinity. When you or other people working on the same pile move larger rocks, the pile can become unstable, causing landslides of large and jagged rocks, so always work at a measured pace, and be alert to the people working above and below you.

- **Take breaks:** Working on mine tailing piles is physically strenuous, so take regular breaks and stay hydrated. On hot summer days, move to a shady area periodically and take a sustained break. Remember that whatever you collect needs to be carried back to your vehicle, so save some energy for your return trip.

- **Wildlife:** When you are hunting in remote areas, and forests in particular, be alert to your surroundings for large or aggressive animals, such as bears, wolves, moose, mountain lions, and, of course, people. We strongly recommend hunting in small groups or at least pairs, and it's important to let people know your planned hunting route and expected return time before going out.

- **Weather:** Weather can change quickly. Plan ahead by getting a current forecast, and then regularly monitor conditions throughout the day. You might want to keep a hooded rain poncho with you, considering the frequency of rain and mist coming off of Lake Superior.

# MINE DUMPS

The copper mines indicated in red on this map have the greatest occurrence of greenstone and datolite. As when hunting copper at a mine site, you must check into the mine's current entrance policy before going in. Start with the Keweenaw Peninsula Chamber of Commerce and local rock clubs.

**Popular Copper Mines for Greenstone and Datolite Hunting**

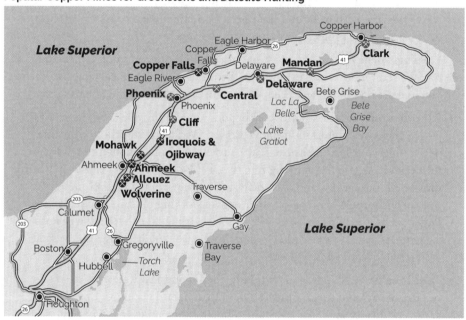

## The Hunting Experience

Whereas a metal detector is your essential tool for finding copper, a 5–30x magnifier and a 30–60x loupe are critical to finding greenstone. While some pieces will be readily identifiable with the naked eye, others will show only the faintest details that allow you to distinguish greenstone from various imposters. And truthfully, many times you won't know in the field because the exterior skin, or husk, of the nodules is just an opaque dark green. You won't find out for sure until you get the nodules back home and do a bit of light grinding or tumbling. Therefore, you need to make sure that you're in a spot where there actually is greenstone.

Do a walk-around on the property to assess which spots might be best suited for hunting. You'll want to find a place where there is a lot of clean rock, as in the first photo above.

- With nothing more than your magnifier in hand, pick a spot and start picking up rocks that appear to have some dark-green material on them.
- Once you've identified a suspect that shows a high probability of being greenstone, continue hunting around in the same spot to see if you find more strong suspects.
- If you find several good pieces, even if they are very small in size, it's time to grab your collecting bucket and tools.

The second and third photos above show two large boulders that are littered with greenstone nodules, some hollow and some with calcite crystal fill. For these, you will need to do some serious hammer and chisel work to break away large chunks of basalt and reduce the mass down to portable pieces.

Above is a nice nodule in a large chunk of basalt. With targeted hammering away from the nodule, a big portion of the basalt can be broken away at the site. For really nice nodules like this one, you'll probably want to finish extracting it from the basalt at your home workshop. Methods for removing the nodules include:

- Hammer and chisel work, especially along seams in the rock
- Sawing away large masses

- Using a grinding disk, or tumbling the pieces after sawing away most of the surrounding rock

Note that as you break down large pieces of rock, you'll undoubtedly expose more nodules inside, and some of them will be better than what was exposed on the outside. So always take time to inspect the inner surfaces as you continue to break away chunks of rock.

Here are some nice nodules in smaller pieces of rock, which only need to be collected and brought home for extraction.

## BEACHES

Beach specimens of greenstone are highly prized because nature has already done the hard work of breaking the nodules free from the host stone and wearing away the thin outer husk. However, finding intact greenstone nodules along the shores of Lake Superior is exceedingly difficult. The stones are softer and more brittle, they are small (or downright tiny), and locations where they can be found are heavily hunted. Some beaches that have been hunted successfully include Eagle River, Esrey Park, Gratiot River, and Pete's. There are privately owned lakefront properties to be found, but remember that you need permission to hunt on private land; we provide some helpful suggestions on this in the Lake Superior Agates chapter (see page 23).

The hunting process is mostly stationary, sitting in areas of the beach with accumulations of lake-tumbled rocks that are pea-size to quarter-size. Scan the top layer of rocks all around you, and then carefully move away the top layer to inspect the rocks beneath. Repeat this process for as many layers as you like. For some hunters, a spray bottle comes in handy because they prefer looking at the color variations when the rocks are wet.

Trying to hunt in the water itself will generally be an exercise in futility, as the specimens are too small to catch sight of through the water. And you'll need to be bending down close enough to see very fine details, so you'll occasionally get splashed by larger waves.

# EXTRACTING GREENSTONE NODULES FROM BASALT AND PERFORMING LAPIDARY WORK

Greenstone is relatively brittle, and it comes in smaller-size nodules that tend to be irregular in shape. Therefore, it is something that will stretch your skills (and patience) if you are just beginning to do lapidary work, so we suggest a bit of practice on larger and harder stones, such as agates, before starting with greenstone.

The finished pieces in the photos below and on the next page were created with a lapidary saw and grinder. See the Thomsonite chapter for how to remove nodules from host rock with a hammer and chisel or with a coring drill. For a comprehensive beginner's guide to the art of lapidary, including information about equipment and supplies, see my book, *Gemstone Tumbling, Cutting, Drilling & Cabochon Making: A Simple Guide to Finishing Rough Stones.*

The lower-right piece shows a greenstone nodule, with some radial eye formations, that might turn out nicely after cutting and grinding away the surface layer and doing some smoothing and shaping.

The host stone is cut so that it's easier to get at the nodule. Subsequent steps included:
- Cutting away the backside material
- Stenciling and shaping the piece into an oval
- Shaping and polishing the top surface

Here's a gorgeous greenstone pendant necklace!

Here's a gorgeous large greenstone nodule with shimmering emerald green crystals around a white calcite-filled center. To create a display of a greenstone nodule inside its host stone, most of the surrounding rock was cut away. Then the top face was ground to a smooth, rounded surface and polished.

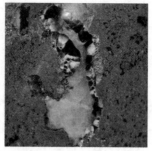
This is a stunning face-polished greenstone display piece!

This is a piece of polished greenstone still in the host stone. The thin outer husk has been gently sanded away to expose the beautiful turtleback pattern. This piece could be removed from the host material and used for jewelry-making or kept as is for display.

## TOOLS AND EQUIPMENT

### General Tools and Equipment

- First aid kit
- 5-gallon buckets
- 5–10x magnifier and a 30–60x loupe
- Heavy-duty pack to carry specimens
- Spray bottle
- Drinking water and nourishing snack foods
- Insect repellent
- Sunscreen
- Packing material such as newspaper or packing paper to wrap any delicate and high-quality specimens

### Clothing Recommendations

- Durable rain gear, as the UP can be rainy and misty
- Supportive and durable hiking and climbing boots
- Safety glasses or face shield since you (and others nearby) might need to break large rocks

- Hat with eye shade

- Non-shaded prescription glasses (if you wear them)—sunglasses reduce your ability to spot subtle color differences

- Heavy-duty work gloves

- Full-length jeans or other work pants, and long shirt sleeves when breaking rocks, to protect against flying rock shards

## Specialty Tools and Equipment

- **Cell phone and service plan that works in the area:** This is a must, especially when in remote areas and working on steep mine tailing piles.

- **Knee and wrist protectors:** For kneeling on hard ground or rock and doing rock hammering and chiseling ($25)

- **5-10x lighted magnifier:** Carson MiniBrite is one good model. These are a must for inspection and identification ($11).

- **30-60x lighted loupe:** Two good makers are Dreame and Jarlink (about $15).

- **Face shield (or safety glasses/goggles):** For protection when breaking rocks ($25)

- **Rock hammer pick:** by Estwing ($30)

- **Chisel of medium width and thickness (flathead screwdrivers can also be used):** by Estwing ($25)

- **Mini sledgehammer:** by Estwing ($35)

- **Rotary tool and diamond cutting bits:** Complete kit with tool and a large set of cutting, grinding, sanding, and polishing heads ($100)

- **Diamond-coated 25mm coring bit:** ($12)

# REFERENCES AND RESOURCES

## Books

- Wilson, Marc L., and Stanley J. Dyl II. *The Michigan Copper Country: The Mineralogical Record March–April 1992.* The Mineralogical Record, 1992.

- Heinrich, E.W. *Minerology of Michigan.* Updated and revised by George W. Robinson. Michigan Technical University, 2004.

- Molloy, Lawrence. *A Guide to Michigan's Historic Keweenaw Copper District.* Great Lakes Geoscience, 2008. (This is an updated version of *Copper Country Road Trips,* with photographs, maps, hidden mines and rock piles, and tours.)

## Shops with Greenstone and Datolite Specimens and Information

- Keweenaw Gem & Gift (also known as Copper Connection), Houghton, MI
  copperconnection.com

- The Wood'n Spoon, Mohawk, MI
  www.facebook.com/TheWoodnSpoon

- Copper World, Calumet, MI
  www.calumetcopper.com

- Quincy Mine, Hancock, MI
  www.quincymine.com

- Red Metal Minerals, Ontonagon, MI
  www.redmetalminerals.com

- Caledonia Mine, Ontonagon, MI
  www.caledoniamine.com

## Facebook Groups and Websites

- Michigan Rocks & Minerals
  www.facebook.com/MichiganRocksandMinerals

- Snob Appeal Jewelry
  www.snobappealjewelry.com/blog/hunting-michigan-greenstones/

## Rock and Mineral Clubs

- Copper Country Rock and Mineral Club
  ccrmc.info

- Ishpeming Rock and Mineral Club
  www.ishpemingrocks.org

## Museums and Educational Institutions

- A. E. Seaman Mineral Museum
  museum.mtu.edu

# LAPIDARY ARTS

This chapter provides an orientation to the tools and processes collectively known as lapidary work and provides some ideas and guidance to the kinds of lapidary products that you can create. For a comprehensive beginner's guide to the art of lapidary, including information about equipment and supplies, see my book, *Gemstone Tumbling, Cutting, Drilling & Cabochon Making: A Simple Guide to Finishing Rough Stones*. It pertains to a wide range of gemstones and fully covers the techniques you need to know.

While many of the gems and minerals in this book show beautifully exactly as found, and may even be more valuable when left as rough or natural specimens, doing some work to enhance their beauty or even make them into jewelry is a natural extension of prospecting and collecting. And some gemstones (notably geodes and whole agate nodules) do not reveal their beauty until they are broken or cut open. But remember that beauty is in the eye of the beholder, and there are no sacred rules about performing lapidary work on any given gemstone!

But first, a note about safety. Good quality safety glasses and hearing protection are essential when working with lapidary machines. Also, anytime you cut or grind rock, dust is created, and **breathing in rock dust can lead to a serious**

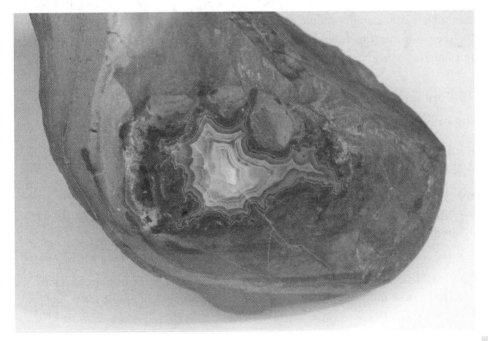

**long-term health condition called silicosis**. Most lapidary processes that create dust, such as sawing or grinding, use water or oil as a lubricant to control the dust, but you can also wear an approved respirator for further protection. For processes that create dust and don't use a lubricant, it is imperative that you wear a respirator and work in a well-ventilated area. An N95 or K95 mask is sufficient unless you are doing heavy grinding for more than an hour.

# TUMBLING

Rock tumbling is generally seen as the "lowest common denominator" of all lapidary work because it has numerous applications and can be adapted to create many different textures, based on your materials or your desired finished products. Tumbling is a process of taking rough stones or cut jewelry pieces and turning them into smooth, high-gloss finished pieces. It is performed using machines known as rock tumblers, of which there are a variety of types and sizes. Most beginners are well advised to start with a small "rotary tumbler," since it is the most cost effective and versatile machine.

Tumbling is a cyclical process, meaning that you'll go through several tumbling "stages" from rough to highly polished. In some cases, you might decide to stop after the pieces are semi-smooth, with finishes sometimes referred to as "satin" or "water-washed." Think of tumbling as something of an art that allows you to create the looks and finishes that you prefer. In fact, you can even purchase a polished stone and "reverse tumble" it to return it to a more natural look and feel. But while tumbling is conceptually simple, only a meticulous attention to detail while following the processes (especially cleaning between tumbling stages) will produce an ultra-high-gloss shine.

## Tumbling Applications and Processes

Rock tumbling can be used for many applications, including:

- Polishing whole stones, or stones that have been chipped or broken, to a high-gloss finish
- Tumbling whole rocks to a natural water-washed or smooth, satin finish
- Tumbling cabochons and pendants in groups to reduce time spent polishing individual pieces
- Removing saw marks from agates or other stones that have been sawed open
- Tumbling rocks that have been ground and shaped on one or more surfaces (called face polishing) to remove "faceting," before polishing the main surface

**Special consideration:** For softer stones, like thomsonite or Petoskey stones, make sure to use softer tumbling media, like basalt or ceramic pellets. Also, run shorter tumbling cycles for these softer stones than you would for harder stones, like agates; sometimes just a couple of hours will be sufficient.

## Tumbling Product Examples

Agates that have been tumbled to a high-gloss shine, an agate that has been tumbled to a smooth and natural water-washed finish, and a piece of copper that has been tumbled to a high-gloss shine

## SAWING

Sawing can be done to cut gemstones in preparation for additional lapidary work, or simply to expose more of the interior beauty of stones such as agates or geodes. While sawing is relatively straightforward, there are techniques and guidelines that will help you get the most out of your gemstone materials. We highly recommend you purchase a saw made specifically for lapidary work, and use saw blades with continuous diamond-coated rims. Also, be sure to follow all manufacturer's instructions and safety guidelines.

### Sawing Applications and Processes

Rock sawing can be used for many applications, including:

- Cutting rocks open to expose their interior is one of the most popular uses of rock saws. For many whole or almost whole agates, the beautiful pattern can only be seen by cutting the rocks open.

- Cutting away rough, unwanted material before face polishing the stones or cutting them into slabs are other ways to use rock saws. Here you try to remove the least amount of material necessary to get a complete and flat surface.

- Cutting slabs or slices for display or for jewelry-making is another method, sometimes "trim cutting" the slices to remove excess material before grinding the pieces to a given shape.

**Special consideration:** Geodes can be cut open using rock saws, but many varieties, including Keokuk geodes, can be damaged by cutting them open rather than chiseling and cracking them open. This is because some of the interior crystal formations might extend across the "cut line" that you choose for sawing, whereas cracking them open only breaks the exterior, or husk, portion of the geode, leaving all of the crystal formations intact.

## Sawing Product Examples

A Teepee Canyon agate that was cut open and then polished on the cut surface

A Lake Superior agate that was cut into slabs and then made into a jewelry pendant

# GRINDING AND POLISHING

Grinding is a way to remove surface material on rough stones, shape stones to a pleasing natural contour, and make jewelry pieces from cut slabs or slices. The pieces are then polished to the desired finish.

There are two primary types of lapidary grinding and polishing machines. For beginners, we strongly recommend flat lapidary grinding and polishing machines because of their low cost, ease of learning, versatility, and portability. Flat lapidary grinders use diamond-coated disks that come in a variety of coarseness levels, or meshes. There is literally no end to the kinds of creations you can make with a flat lapidary grinding machine, and you can develop skills quickly. Some more-advanced lapidary artists use vertical-wheel arbor grinding machines, but these come at 3 to 4 times the cost of the flat disk machines.

## Grinding and Polishing Product Examples

Face polished prairie agate (high gloss)

Face polished Lake Superior agate (high gloss)

Face polished Lake Superior agate (satin finish)

Lake Superior agate cabochon (high gloss)

# PETOSKEY STONE POLISHING

Because there are special processes and supplies needed for polishing Petoskey stones that aren't covered in most lapidary publications, we decided to go into a bit more depth and offer different options. Many people mistakenly assume Petoskeys can be tumbled just like agates, only to find their treasures crumbled or badly damaged. Since Petoskey stones are very soft (a 3 on the Mohs mineral hardness scale), they generally need to be worked by hand. This can be a laborious and lengthy process, taking 1 to 3 hours per stone, depending on the size and condition of the stone. We provide three methods for polishing Petoskeys on the next page. Regardless of the method used, we strongly recommend using stones with darker tan or gray shading and well-defined patterns, and surfaces with minimal or no pitting.

## Polishing with a Flat Lapidary Grinder and Polisher (fast and easy)

This method takes 15 to 30 minutes for medium-size Petoskey stones 2"–4" in diameter. You'll start with a 325 mesh sanding disk and work the area of the stone you want to polish—anywhere from a single flat "face" to the whole stone. After you have a consistent finish across the area you sanded, you'll perform the same operation with the 600 mesh and then the 1200 mesh disks. By the time you're done with the 1200 mesh disk, you'll have a glossy finish. To get an ultra-high-gloss finish, you'll use a polishing disk and diamond polishing paste.

## Polishing with a Handheld Rotary Tool (fast and relatively easy)

This method takes 20 to 60 minutes. The first and most important note about this method is that you'll be dry sanding, so you must wear an approved respirator mask and protective eyewear. You also need to watch your fingertips when working with a rotary tool, just as with any power sanding or grinding tool. You'll use 60, 120, and 240 mesh disks in succession to grind the surfaces of the stone that you want polished. After that you'll use 800, 1500, and 3000 grit wet-sanding papers and sand by hand. Next, rub the stone vigorously with a 3M Trizact 5000 pad as a pre-polish step, and finally, sprinkle sub-micron aluminum oxide polishing compound on a wet piece of denim cloth and rub to a high-gloss polish.

## Polishing by Hand (painstakingly slow and laborious, but cheap)

This method takes 1 to 3 hours per stone. You'll need 4 to 12 different grades or grits of wet-sanding paper. The most common are 80, 220, 400, 600, and 1200 grit. Use finer and finer sanding paper. Some people finish with a polishing cloth and 14,000 diamond polishing compound. The 80 grit takes the longest, as it is the grit needed to remove all surface pits. You might be able to skip this step entirely if you start with stones that are already free of pits and uniformly smooth to the touch.

## Polished Petoskey Stone Example

A rough and dry Petoskey stone as found

The same stone when wet

The same stone after polishing

# COPPER CLEANING AND POLISHING

Some pieces of float copper, such as weathered specimens found along the shores of Lake Superior, can be tumble polished, but pieces like copper crystals or float copper with heavier layers of oxidation require special treatments. There aren't a lot of published guides to cleaning or polishing copper, so we've included a short how-to section, and we think you'll agree that it illustrates why copper is prized and valued by modern-day prospectors.

## Cleaning

Most native copper specimens are found with natural oxidization layers and discolorations, and there also might be calcite crystal formations that obscure the copper crystals. These specimens can be made more presentable with cleaning or chemical treatments. Just as with other gems and minerals, high-quality copper specimens should be treated carefully, and you should always use the least aggressive method for cleaning and preparing them for display. This is sometimes referred to as the "do-no-harm principle."

Many of the most beautiful and valuable copper crystal specimens have been cleaned up using only water and stiff-bristle nylon brushes (note that wire brushes can scratch your specimens), and even these have been applied carefully to avoid damage. Methods that involve the use of strong acids and chemicals can **permanently damage and destroy copper surfaces**. Therefore, the cleaning processes outlined below proceed from least to most aggressive, and you should only use the latter methods after careful consideration. When in doubt, talk with someone that has experience and knows the relative value of native copper specimens. The process we present below is "progressive"; at the end of each step, consider carefully whether any further work will truly improve your specimens.

## Cleaning Equipment and Supplies

- Pressure washer (especially for large specimens)
- Mini picks and hooks
- Hammer
- Vinegar, flour, salt
- Muriatic acid
- Copper polishing product, such as Copper Brite
- Clear lacquer spray

- All work must be done outdoors and away from pets, young children, and automobiles.

- If you notice any foaming and bubbling, especially if there are visible fumes, you could be exposed to poisonous gases—you must cease work immediately and carefully dilute and rinse your specimens thoroughly.

- Protective clothing is a must, including eye goggles that provide a seal around your eyes and chemical-resistant rubber gloves and apron.

- Have running water or some other water supply close at hand to dilute and rinse spills; water is the safest neutralizer, rather than other chemicals.

- Always keep your acid solutions in clearly labeled and tightly sealed containers, and keep them in a place that cannot be reached or accessed by young children.

## Process Details

Use a hammer to break away larger chunks of host rock and expose more of the copper. Sometimes you might put some sand on top of the specimen to cushion the hammer blows when you are working on potentially higher-grade specimens.

Use a stiff-bristle nylon brush and warm water to remove any large concentrations of dirt and loose rock fragments; you can also use a mini pick to get stubborn pieces out of pits and crevices.

For medium or large specimens, use a pressure washer to remove the remaining dirt and small rock fragments.

If you want to clean your specimen further, start with one of the vinegar methods before deciding whether to then use chemicals. However, if there are calcite crystals that you want to remove because they are obscuring the copper crystals, you'll need to use the muriatic acid method in order to dissolve them.

- **Vinegar soak:** Fill a container with vinegar sufficient to immerse your copper specimens. Place your specimens in the vinegar, and allow to soak for 24 hours. Remove the specimens and scrub with a nylon brush or toothbrush. You can repeat this multiple times if you continue to see progress in exposing the copper.

- **Vinegar paste:** Create a mixture of flour, salt, and vinegar, and then apply it onto all of the surfaces you want to clean. A good starting point is ½ cup of flour and a teaspoon of salt, and then stir in the vinegar until you get a paste. Leave the paste on the specimen for 10 minutes, and then thoroughly rinse with water and lightly scrub with a nylon brush. You can perform this process 1 to 3 times before deciding on whether to use muriatic acid.

- **Muriatic acid soak:** After putting on your rubber gloves, pour enough muriatic acid (also known as hydrochloric acid) to immerse your specimen into a sturdy ceramic or plastic bowl. Gently place your specimen into the acid. Allow the specimen to soak for 10 to 15 minutes, then remove it and rinse with water while gently scrubbing with a nylon brush. You can repeat this step 1 to 3 times, but do not let the specimens soak for more than 30 minutes each time. If the muriatic acid isn't too cloudy, you can put it back into a sealed container to reuse later. If you are ready to dispose of it, you'll need to bring it to a household hazardous waste collection site.

Optional steps to further brighten the specimen and preserve it (note that for premium crystal specimens, these are not typically recommended).

- Wearing rubber gloves, rub the areas of the specimen you wish to highlight with Copper Brite or another copper cleaning solution and a soft cloth.
- Rinse the specimen and dry it with a soft cloth.
- Let it air dry for 10 minutes.
- Spray the specimen with clear, acrylic lacquer for preservation.

Here is a specimen that was cleaned using a vinegar soak. Note how the vinegar has turned green from removal of the copper oxidization layers.

## Polishing

Polishing is typically only done on float copper. Generally, you'll be trying to create an aesthetic presentation of polished sections offset by natural or rough surfaces. The bright-green oxidation on a premium specimen is nicely offset by polishing portions of the surface to a high-gloss reddish-orange or copper-colored finish. In shops throughout the UP, these pieces are sometimes referred to as "butchite." Unfortunately, there is no documented evidence as to why or when this term originated.

## Polishing Equipment and Supplies

- Pressure washer (especially for large specimens)
- Flat lapidary grinder
- Silicon carbide abrasive disks for the lapidary grinder, at 40 or 60 mesh, 100 mesh, and 400 mesh. Note: Don't use diamond disks because copper residue will gum them up quickly and ruin them. Silicon carbide-coated disks will gum up, as well, but they are only about 20% of the cost of diamond disks.
- Polishing disk and polishing compound
- Clear lacquer spray (optional)

## Process Details

Use a stiff-bristle nylon brush and warm water to remove any large concentrations of dirt and loose rock fragments.

For medium or large specimens, use a pressure washer to remove the remaining dirt from pits and crevices.

Inspect the surface of the specimen to determine what natural colors and features you want to preserve and where you want to polish. Keep in mind that any dips or pits that are greater than 1/8" can't be completely ground out.

You can draw a rough outline on the surface of the area you want to polish using a marker, since you will grind away the markings.

Using a lapidary grinder, you will grind away the selected area of the surface oxidation and then sand, smooth, and polish in the sequence outlined below:

- Using the 40 or 60 mesh disk or wheel, begin grinding in the middle of the area that you outlined, and work outwards to the marked outline until you have ground away the entire target area and you have a smooth and rounded surface.
- Perform rough sanding with a 100 mesh disk or wheel until there are no visible scratches.
- Perform fine sanding with a 400 mesh disk or wheel until there is a smooth, satin finish and a light glow.
- Perform polishing with the polishing disk and diamond polishing compound.
- Use a cloth rag to thoroughly clean the surface of any loose polishing compound or grit; optionally use a buffing or polishing compound on the rag.
- Spray or rub the surface with clear lacquer to inhibit oxidization.

This is a nice smaller-size piece of float copper with colorful green oxidization. Grinding and polishing were done on the less colorful portion to expose and then polish the bright-orange copper.

This specimen has copper flecks in quartz. A portion of the stone was polished to highlight both the copper and the quartz, which provides a nice contrast to the rough stone.

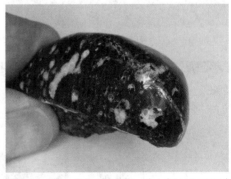

A nice shot copper specimen with some small copper beads or "shot," some mixed copper and quartz nodules, and a vein of copper and quartz running laterally across the stone. Grinding and polishing was done on the portion of the stone with the most interesting and visible copper inclusions; the rest of the stone is left rough as a natural offset to the polished surface.

# Professional Copper Polishing Process and Examples

Two nice larger-size pieces of float copper, about 4 pounds each

First, the ends are sawed off so that the display pieces can stand as desired. Note that copper requires notched-rim diamond blades, which are much riskier to use and generally not recommended for beginners.

Grinding on 40 mesh, 100 mesh, and 400 mesh wheels as described on page 238

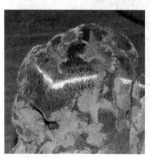

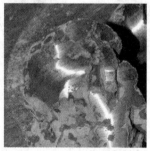

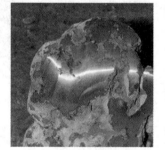

Photos taken after 40 mesh, 100 mesh, and 400 mesh wheels

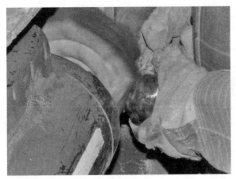

At the polishing and buffing wheel

After it's done there's a high-gloss shine but still some black copper residue to be removed.

Chemical cleaning to remove the black residue; not recommended for beginners

Spraying all sides of the piece with clear lacquer maintains the high-gloss shine and also the natural bright-green oxidation on the unpolished portion.

The best of both worlds—natural and polished

A gorgeous example of a cut slab of float copper that has been ground, polished, and sprayed with clear lacquer

## Copper Crystal Etching and Splash Copper

There are two additional lapidary works that can be done with copper; both of these are advanced applications, but they are worth mentioning. The first is called "etching" and uses aggressive acid solutions such as sulfamic acid to remove calcite from copper crystals, leaving just the fully formed crystal formations. The second involves creating pure copper pieces called "splash copper." Molten copper is poured onto a flat surface, allowed to harden, and then ground and polished with handheld grinding and buffing tools.

## ADDITIONAL LAPIDARY PROCESSES

There are many other lapidary processes that you can learn and apply to the gems and minerals in this book, such as drilling, metalsmithing, cabochon making, and jewelry-making. Many hobbyists consider lapidary work to be a valuable extension of their rockhounding pursuits. We encourage you to do join a rock club, where you can meet and learn from other lapidary experts.

## LAPIDARY SUPPLIERS

This list is just a starting point for finding full-service lapidary equipment and supply vendors, and also vendors that sell specimens of the rocks and minerals featured in this book. We recommend finding a supplier who you can visit in person because you'll get an opportunity to see many of the machines in use with hands-on demonstrations, and you're more likely to get what you need rather than something that is beyond your needs or unable to perform the kinds of tasks you want to do. eBay is included since it is also a great source for used equipment and for both rough and finished specimens of all types of rocks and minerals.

- Minnesota Lapidary Supply, Princeton, MN
  lapidarysupplies.com
- Kingsley North, Norway, MI
  kingsleynorth.com
- The Gem Shop, Cedarburg, WI
- Keweenaw Gem & Gift (also known as Copper Connection), Houghton, MI
  copperconnection.com
- Rio Grande
  www.riogrande.com

- The Rock Shed, Keystone, SD
  therockshed.com

- eBay.com

# REFERENCES AND RESOURCES

## Books

- Magnuson, Jim. *Gemstone Tumbling, Cutting, Drilling and Cabochon Making: A Simple Guide to Finishing Rough Stones.* Adventure Publications, 2015

## Facebook Groups

- Lapidary Tips & Tricks
  www.facebook.com/groups/774419732663040

## Magazines

- *Rock & Gem Magazine*

# METAL DETECTING

This chapter provides general information on how to select and use metal detectors to find precious metals in their natural state, such as gold, copper, and silver. If you want a detector that is also good for hunting coins, artifacts, and jewelry, see the references provided at the end of this chapter. All of the detectors we recommend can certainly be used for hunting these other things, but they may not be the best fit if those items will be your primary "targets," and you might be able to get by with a significantly cheaper machine.

If you've never used a metal detector before, you'll quickly find out that there's a dizzying array of choices, and you can quickly become confused with terminology like Very Low Frequency (VLF), Pulse Induction (PI), Discrimination, and Threshold. Additionally, you'll find out that there are machines that cost well over $5,000! These ultra-high-end machines will have enticing ads that say things like "Hunt like the pros." The information below will help guide beginners in making a sensible investment, and you can start having success using these machines with discipline and a small amount of practice—much less, in fact, than if you purchase one of the more sophisticated detectors. If your metal detecting and prospecting passion grows, and you want a more flexible and powerful machine, your original detector(s) can always be used by friends and family members when you go out prospecting together!

It does take a considerable amount of time to become comfortable and confident in using your metal detector. It can easily take you 100 hours of field usage before you truly become "one with your machine," and this will only happen if you take the time to first learn about the machine and perform "designed tests" with your detector.

# SELECTING A METAL DETECTOR

Since this is a book for beginning prospectors, we only present machines and accompanying features in the low-to-middle area of the price range. With today's technology, you can rest assured that any machine we recommend will do its task quite capably when used for gold, silver, and copper prospecting. All of the machines on our list are the Very Low Frequency (VLF) type, since Pulse Induction (PI) machines are considerably more expensive and complex. An experienced prospector could still be very productive with one of these detectors—more so than a beginner using higher-end machines.

## Metal Detector Feature Definitions

The following definitions of metal detector features are non-technical and mostly focused on how they'll affect your experience in using the machines. They will help you understand what you are evaluating and provide a jump-start into learning about and using your new metal detector.

- **Operating frequency:** A lower frequency number is better for deeper ground penetration, whereas a higher number is better for finding very small pieces. For copper, a lower number such as 5–10 kHz is perfectly fine, but if you also want to hunt for small gold nuggets and flakes, you'll need to be in the 15–75 kHz range.

- **Audio target identification:** This is the ability of the detector to gauge the size and type of metal for a given object. A good starter machine will be able to distinguish aluminum, iron, copper, silver, gold, lead, and more while also giving an indication of size. When you are using the "All Metal" mode for discrimination, this will give you a good clue on whether the item is worth digging out.

- **Multiple tones:** This means that you'll get progressively higher tones from more-valuable targets, like gold and silver, and lower tones for things like lead or aluminum. Some machines provide options for how you want the tones broken out, such as into a 3-tone or 7-tone scale, whereas Multiple Tones provides the maximum breakdown and scale for all types of metals and objects.

- **Discrimination options (all metal or discriminate):** Discrimination is the ability to screen out certain types of metal, like iron and aluminum. When you are using Discriminate, it reduces the depth at which you can find things. With both options in a detector, you can start with the All Metal setting and then switch to Discriminate and see if you're still getting a signal. After a while, you'll get the hang of deciding when it's "worth the dig" based on what the machine is telling you.

- **Ground balance options (manual/fixed or auto):** If you're detecting in areas with high mineralization (such as black sand when hunting for gold, or iron when hunting in copper country), you'll get a lot of "ground chatter," which can be quite distracting and even mask the good signals. You can start with the automatic setting and let the machine decide how much masking it should do, or you can set the ground balancing level on your machine manually, run for a while, and then periodically readjust. However, many experienced gold prospectors prefer the Manual, or Fixed, mode, because the Automatic mode can filter out smaller targets by confusing them with ground mineralization, exactly what you don't want with small gold nuggets and flakes! With manual setting, or "tuning," you'll choose a spot and then raise and lower the coil from lightly touching the ground to about 3 inches above the ground; you then gradually adjust the ground balance setting until there is minimal ground chatter. When you are on familiar hunting grounds, you might have very specific settings that produce the best results.

- **Sensitivity/Gain:** In general, the Sensitivity setting controls the depth and size of the items that the detector will seek and how strongly it will register an audible signal. If you're in an area near power lines and transformers or telecommunications towers, or if the ground is heavily mineralized, you might need to reduce the sensitivity in order to reduce chatter. When you're first getting started or prospecting in a new or unfamiliar area, you are best to set for greater sensitivity. You'll get more trash at first and deal with more chatter, but you won't miss out on good-quality finds that are smaller or at greater depth. This is even more important in areas where there might have been a lot of prior metal detecting activity, as the easy-to-detect items have most likely already been found. And it's also important for gold, since gold nuggets of significant value can be pea-size or smaller, whereas with copper you're generally not interested in things less than the weight of a quarter.

- **Threshold level:** There is an audible background hum that results from naturally mineralized ground. Usually you should set the Threshold level so that it's just audible, because if it's too loud it might mask faint signals from smaller or deeper targets. Threshold can also be helpful to let you know when you're moving too quickly, as it will "drop out" or stop producing the audible hum.

- **Depth indicator:** This is a reading of probable depth for the item the detector has located. Accuracy can vary wildly, so be sure to check for the item in the material you dig out, especially if the depth reading was greater than 3 or 4 inches.

- **Pinpoint mode:** You'll turn Pinpoint Mode on after identifying a target to help you zero in on exactly where the item is beneath the coil. This is helpful with larger-size coils, or in areas that you need to be especially careful not to disturb too much of the ground, such as on someone's lawn.

- **Pinpoint handheld detector:** This small metal detector that's usually about a foot long is used for locating items in the material you've dug out. These handy devices are indispensable and well worth the additional investment. They often come bundled with regular metal detectors at a considerable discount from individual purchase prices.

- **Visual identification LCD screen:** An LCD screen provides digital readouts of your current settings and information about any items it identifies, such as type of metal and relative size.

- **Coil size:** A larger coil allows you to cover more ground faster and at greater depth. A smaller coil allows you to do more precise positioning, and they are more maneuverable, which means they can get into tighter spaces.

**Metal Detector Features**

| Features and Options | Details and Value/Importance |
| --- | --- |
| Operating Frequency Between 15 kHz and 75 kHz | Critical for gold nuggets |
| Audio Target Identification | At least 3–5 tones for different kinds of items |
| Discrimination—All Metal and Discriminate Modes | Need both modes |
| Ground Balance Options—Manual or Auto | Manual is critical for gold nuggets |
| Sensitivity/Gain Adjustment | High value in heavily mineralized areas, places with lots of trash, and places where you want to skip over smaller-size targets, such as very small copper pieces |
| Threshold Setting | Important general feature |
| Depth Indicator | Moderate value; signal strength (audio or visual) will guide you as well |
| Pinpoint Mode | High value, especially for deeper targets |
| Visual Identification LCD Screen | Valuable for getting visual feedback in addition to audio feedback and for confirming your settings |
| Waterproof Coil | Fully submersible is great, since you never know what conditions you might be hunting in |
| Water-Resistant Detector | Can be out in rain |
| Search Coil Shape | Round is preferred, but other options are OK |
| Search Coil of 9" or 10" diameter | This is the general or all-purpose standard |
| NiMH Rechargeable Battery Option | Strongly prefer because of longer life in field use |
| Telescoping Shaft | Helps in situations where it's difficult to position the detector head on a level plane to your target |
| Coil Guard Attachments | Critical for rough-surface detecting |

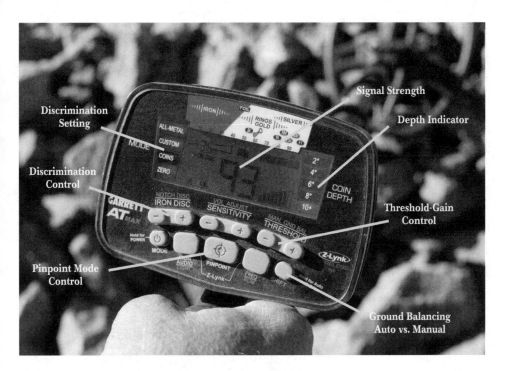

# Metal Detector Selection Requirements

Below is the list of critical features, with some brief notes and further details to consider. All of the detector makes and models that we recommend meet or exceed these requirements.

## Suggested Makes and Models

Minelab X-Terra 305 ($260)

Minelab X-Terra 705 ($500)

Fisher Gold Bug 2 ($700)

Garrett Ace 400 ($340)

Garrett AT Gold ($640)

Garrett AT Max ($725)

Whites GoldMaster GMT 24K ($730)

Garrett Pro-Pointer AT–handheld* ($150)

   * We only recommend this one handheld pinpoint detector; it is a popular and
   well-respected make and model.

# GETTING STARTED WITH YOUR NEW METAL DETECTOR

Below is a concise set of steps that will save a lot of frustration and the missed opportunities that result from learning on the fly. While we strongly recommend that you follow these steps, we also recommend that beginners spend some time learning by trial and error. A person can easily get too focused on toying with and adjusting machine settings, so to start with, don't set things like sensitivity or discrimination too aggressively in an attempt to minimize the amount of junk or heavily mineralized "hot rocks" that you find. It's good that you get to know the imposters firsthand and learn to distinguish them from genuine targets. And it's critical that you learn and become intimately familiar with "the voice" of your metal detector.

- **Read your owner's manual and watch available videos on using your detector to find the kinds of metals you'll be prospecting for.** This is important because technology is constantly changing, and each machine has different settings and instrumentation.

- Write down the settings that you'll use for the given metal types and the configurations you'll use for testing (small gold nuggets, float copper masses, etc.), and also for the conditions that you'll be hunting in (mine tailing piles, underground, in running water, etc.). We provide a sample outline for dynamic tuning and ground balancing on the next page.

- Obtain a set of sample raw metal pieces of different sizes that are representative of what you'll be hunting for, such as gold flakes and nuggets, copper crystals, copper in matrix, and float copper. Also put together a set of common junk items, like nails, aluminum cans, wire.

- Set your machine to the test settings you wrote down.

- Place your sample metal specimens in real-to-life settings, but first place them in a container so that your samples don't get lost, especially any gold pieces! Be sure to use a container that doesn't affect the performance of your metal detector, such as a glass or plastic vial or a durable zip-top bag.

- Perform your tests, and document the results, making note of any difficulties you had and any adjustments you made to your machine settings while doing the tests. These settings can be used as a baseline for the specific kinds of things you'll be hunting for and the conditions in the areas that you'll visit most frequently.

- If you had significant difficulties finding the specimens and made adjustments during the test, or if you found out about different settings through further research, update your test plans and re-run the tests.

- Once you get out on a real hunt, run the same tests in the actual environment. Things like ground mineralization and depth or density of the materials you are detecting in and through can cause substantial variations in your results, and you might need to do some further adaptations. Take the time to write these down for future reference!

After many years of using your metal detector, you might forget about the learning curve you had with your now trusty and familiar machine. If you eventually decide to switch or upgrade to a new detector, plan to go through the same "burn in" process with your new machine. Many a metal detecting enthusiast has been heard saying, "I wish I had just kept my old machine." After years of use you'll have learned many new tricks and adaptations for your specific usage scenarios, and every machine is different, especially with constantly changing technology. So do NOT buy a brand-new detector a week before you go on a major prospecting expedition! Or if you do, at least bring along "old reliable," in case you have difficulty getting accustomed to the new machine.

## Metal Detector Tuning and Setup

This is how to perform "dynamic tuning," the most common method of detector tuning and manual ground balancing. **But once again, we strongly advise you to read the owner's manual for your machine, since each machine has different controls and instrumentation.**

- Set machine to All Metal mode.
- Set the ground balance control at the midpoint.
- Set Sensitivity to about 75%.
- Rotate Threshold control until a constant background hum is barely audible.
- Move the coil over the ground until you are over a "clean spot" (low ground mineralization)—you won't be picking up any signals or "noise."
- Keeping the coil parallel to the ground, raise and lower it slowly, from just touching the surface to about 3" above the surface. If the Threshold audio increases while lowering the coil, you should reduce the ground balance; if it increases while raising the coil, you should increase the ground balance. Continue doing this until there is no change to the Threshold audio as you raise and lower the coil.
- Increase the Sensitivity level to just below the point at which the detector's performance becomes unstable (as shown by an inconsistency of the Threshold hum). You want a consistent low-level hum without excessive noise, or chatter.

# A Few Key Usage Tips

- Speed kills! Use a slow "sweep speed" when looking for smaller and deeper targets; you might find this difficult, but you should try for about 10 seconds for a full side-to-side sweep of about 8 feet. Overlap your coil sweeps by 25–50%, since the center point of the coil gives the best results. You might think you are moving at a snail's pace, and you are, but the metal detecting "tortoise" will definitely bring home more gold!

- Keep the coil close to or even touching the ground, especially for small gold pieces.

- A more expensive machine doesn't always equal better results.

- Detailed recording of your results leads to better outcomes (where you hunted–exactly, detector settings, what you found, whether there are additional places to try in the same location–think quadrants or sections).

- Headphones are great if you are around other people detecting, and they produce a truer sound than the built-in speaker. However, they might not be needed for large-target prospecting, like copper, they can be a hassle to put on and off, and they'll mute other external noises you might not want to miss–like Sasquatch sneaking up behind you!

Ground balancing before starting your hunt: Gradually raise and lower the coil, making adjustments until the Threshold audio is stable and at a low hum.

Threshold setting can be more finely tuned with headphones.

The Pinpoint feature gives a more precise location of the target beneath the center of the coil. You can also get a depth reading at this point, and then use your handheld pinpointer tool to zero in. As you dig out material, set it carefully to the side in one place, in case the target specimen comes out with the material you are digging in. The pinpointer tool will confirm that you've successfully retrieved the target item.

Wide sweeps are important when you're covering a lot of ground. Be methodical in moving through the area that you're hunting in, and consider making small markings with foot drags or some kind of marker such as a small flag to keep track of where you've been.

## REFERENCES AND RESOURCES

### Books

- Ralph, Chris. *Fists Full of Gold: How You Can Find Gold in the Mountains and Deserts.* Published by Chris Ralph, 2010.
- Smith, Mark. *Metal Detecting: A Beginner's Guide.* CreateSpace Independent Publishing Platform, 2014.

### Facebook Groups

- Metal Detecting U.S. Only
  www.facebook.com/groups/USDETECTING

# GLOSSARY

**Alluvial:** Material that has been moved and deposited by running water.

**Banding:** Banding is the most common term used to describe the recurring patterns that are found in all varieties of agates. The most common banding configuration is known as "fortification" banding; it features concentric bands that roughly follow the outside shape of an agate, as the walls do around a fort. Other types of banding include gravitational (or water-level) banding and spherical eye formations.

**Bench gravel or deposit:** Material found up the valley slope from a stream that was deposited when the stream used to run at that higher level.

**Black sand:** Fine granules of magnetite and hematite that can be removed from a gold pan with a magnet.

**Botryoidal:** When mineral formations feature rounded bumps, similar to a bunch of grapes.

**Bucket scope:** A 5-gallon bucket with the bottom cut out and replaced by a piece of sturdy plexiglass. This is a helpful tool for looking at underwater rocks in shallow areas.

**Claim:** A legally obtained and documented right to hunt for, extract, and process specific gems and minerals on a specific piece of legally defined property. This only refers to gold in this book.

**Core drilling:** Small and delicate gemstones like thomsonite and greenstone sometimes need to be removed or extracted from bedrock using a diamond-coated core drill. The result is a tubular-shaped core with the gemstone still inside. Subsequent grinding and tumbling is performed to free the gemstone from the host stone.

**Druzy:** A coating of fine sugar-like crystals.

**Eluvial:** This refers to material that has been weathered free from its host but is still near its source.

**Etching:** Copper crystal specimens are often surrounded by calcite. To expose the copper crystals without damaging them, the specimens can be soaked in solutions, such as sulfamic acid. Special handling procedures must be followed diligently to avoid burning the skin and eyes.

**Extraction:** The process by which you gather and remove material from dry land or from rivers and streams for purposes of separating out the gems or minerals you are seeking.

**Float copper:** Copper masses that weathered out of bedrock and that were subsequently ground down and naturally "tumbled" by glacial activity and erosion. These masses range from less than an ounce to several thousand pounds, and they can be found hundreds of miles away from the Keweenaw Peninsula where they originated. Float copper is great for polishing and for making it into free-standing display pieces or things like bookends.

**Geode cracking:** Using tools to split a geode into two pieces, revealing the crystals inside.

**Glacial till:** Massive deposits of sand and gravel that were freed from their host rock by weathering and moved by glacial activities. These deposits are sometimes spread in thin layers across hundreds of square miles, and sometimes they are more than 100 feet deep in concentrated areas. Sand and gravel pits south and west of Lake Superior are generally located where there are massive deposits of glacial till.

**Host rock:** Most of the gems and minerals covered in this book were formed inside of another kind of host rock, such as basalt or quartz, and were weathered out by natural forces or extracted with commercial mining and processing equipment and processes.

**Hunting:** The activity that follows prospecting in which you search for and collect the gems and minerals you are seeking, and in some cases, perform pre-processing (especially for gold).

**Imposter:** Any rock or mineral that visually mimics a more precious gem or mineral. Some people refer to imposters as "teasers" or "foolers."

**Inclusions:** Some gemstones contain other minerals in addition to their primary chemical composition. For example, agates sometimes have copper inclusions that replace a portion of their quartz material; this variety of agates is extremely rare and valuable.

**Lapidary:** A broad term that includes a long list of processes for enhancing the beauty or usefulness of the gems and minerals that you collect. The most common activities are cutting and polishing gems and minerals for display or for jewelry-making.

**Locale:** Localized prospecting and hunting sites that might encompass several square miles at most.

**Lode gold:** The gold that is still embedded within the host stone where it formed. Most lode gold forms in quartz veins within bedrock masses. This is why gold prospectors always look for telltale quartz and quartzite stones.

**Mesh (disks, wheels, grit):** Abrasives for grinding and polishing gemstones range from very coarse to very fine. The coarseness of the abrasives is measured and described with a mesh rating. The most-coarse abrasives are 40–80 mesh, and the finest, for polishing, are 14,000 mesh.

**Mohs hardness:** A scale that ranks the hardness of minerals. The softest mineral is talc, with a rating of 1, and the hardest is diamond, at 10. To obtain a high polish, stones usually need a hardness rating of at least 5. Agates have a hardness rating of 7, for example.

**Native:** A geology term that refers to a mass of a pure or almost pure element, not combined with other minerals, such as a mass of native copper.

**Nodule:** Agates and other gemstones often form as nodules (small, usually rounded masses) in "vesicles," or air pockets, inside of host bedrock masses, such as basalt or rhyolite. Other gemstones that form as nodules include thomsonite and greenstone.

**Placer gold:** Gold that has weathered out of the host quartz and bedrock in the form of either gold particulates or gold nuggets. All of the gold prospecting activities in this book are for placer gold.

**Prospecting:** An activity specifically for finding accessible locations to productively hunt for and collect gems and minerals and acquire authorization to do so. Prospecting needs to be done continually to find new locales, as old favorites get depleted or become restricted.

**Rattler:** A type of geode with a thin outer shell and some crystals inside that have broken loose, resulting in a rattling sound when shaken.

**Regions:** Large geographical areas that contain many potential hunting locales.

**Signer:** A term used by Fairburn agate hunters to describe very small agate banding sections with only 1–3 banding rings visible in a large piece of host jasper or limestone. While these are technically Fairburn agates, they are not nearly as beautiful or valuable as Fairburns with numerous bands or fortifications with alternating colors.

**Sluicing:** The primary method for separating gold from a large volume of pay dirt and sand. Sluices come in numerous configurations, such as a manual stream sluice or an engine-powered sluice.

**Solid geode:** A geode that doesn't have a hollow center or cavity with crystal formations. Solid geodes are not as beautiful as those with crystal formations and are considered "junk" by most hunters and collectors. They are also heavier for their size, so they can often be distinguished even without breaking them open.

**Tailings:** Commercial mining operations discard large volumes of waste rock that is considered to have minimal or insufficient amounts of the desired mineral they are after. This waste rock is usually left in large piles. Hobbyists can often find good-quality specimens of copper crystals or gold nuggets in mine tailings.

**Tuning a metal detector:** Metal detectors have an array of settings and instrumentation that can be "tuned" for optimal use based on the kinds of things you are hunting for, the amount of other metallic mineralization in the ground, the probability of junk objects (bottle caps, nails, etc.), the size and depth of the specimens you expect to find, and other factors.

**UV flashlight filter:** Some UV Flashlights have a filtering lens in front of the UV light diodes. The filtering reduces the amount of light "noise" and helps to bring focus onto the source of fluorescent light reflection.

**Venue:** The specific terrain, setting, or conditions where materials will be inspected and hunted for gemstones and minerals. Shorelines, farm fields, and gravel pits are examples of venues.

**Zeolite:** Zeolites are silica-based crystal formations that display ultrafine needle fans that are frequently in a full spherical configuration or eye. Thomsonite is a member of the zeolite family.

# FIELD NOTES

# ACKNOWLEDGMENTS

This book would not be possible without the passion and dedication of many amazing field experts. Their level of expertise and ability to patiently explain critical details about both the prospecting and hunting processes is truly invaluable. While I had previously hunted for many of the gems and minerals in this book, my success rates were somewhere between fair and poor. By the end of my field research trips with these experts, I was finding things that I would have previously missed. One last note is that all of these people shared their knowledge generously, and they are a tribute to rockhounding in the 21$^{st}$ century!

**Ryan Lauzon and Michael Bruce:** Fairburn and Scenic black agate; Ryan (far left) has an intense depth of knowledge and experience with hunting Fairburn agates. He also has an innate skill for conveying his knowledge in a way and at a level that is appropriate for his audience. If there's a Fairburn agate to be found when Ryan is on the hunt, you can be sure he'll be bringing it home. Ryan's girlfriend and daughter are also awesome agate hunters, and they work incredibly well together as a hunting team!

Mike (second from right) is a relative newcomer to the Fairburn agate hunting world, but he has an intense passion for hunting this incredibly elusive gem. Mike taught me to get down on my hands and knees and notice the smallest clues. He also has two wonderful children and good friends that love hunting for agates, and they have a crazy rock "hound" named Sadie!

**Erik Rasmussen:** Thomsonite; Erik is what some people might call a "Renaissance man." If I were to list all of his talents and skills, it would take another book! When I started on this book I didn't think we'd be able to include thomsonite because I thought the source was depleted. Erik taught me about going to the bedrock source for thomsonite and how to skillfully extract and process it down to high-grade jewelry stones. Also, Erik's photography talent shows up in the book, as all of the action-related photos in the Thomsonite chapter are his work. If you check in with Erik during the winter, you might just find him out running his dogsled team!

**Bryan Holst (Noodle):** Keokuk geodes; Bryan, or Noodle as he likes to be called, has a true gift for finding geode hotspots and for making the most out of the various geode hunting venues. Like the other field experts, he does an amazing job of keeping a running dialogue going about all of the prospecting and hunting details. I think if you cracked my head open at the end of our amazing field experience, you would have found geode crystals! Noodle is just a wonderful person and an awesome guide.

**Don Hamm:** South Dakota gold; There is very little about gold that Don doesn't know! He has been around gold since he was a small child, and it got deep in his veins. So he knows a LOT about the history of gold in western South Dakota, but his knowledge of modern-day prospecting, hunting, and processing is just as deep. Don showed me an endless array of methods and tools, but he kept things focused on beginner-level skills. Don loves helping people get started in gold prospecting and has been the president of the Black Hills Prospecting Club for many years. Spend a day on a gold claim with Don, and you'll come home with gold in the pan, burning to get back out for another hunt!

**Steve Olson:** Copper and silver, greenstone and datolite, metal detecting; Steve has an amazing array of talents and interests. His interests in rockhounding span a huge number of gems and minerals, and the geographies where they are found. But Steve's true passion is for copper. This photo shows him holding a copper crystal formation that has been displayed at the A. E. Seaman Mineral Museum in Houghton, MI, a museum that holds the most valuable and prized copper specimens in the world! Steve is also an excellent lapidary artist. And Steve is a modern-day metal detecting guru. After three days of tromping around the Keweenaw Peninsula with Steve, both my body and mind had been stretched to the max, and it's an experience I'll always treasure!

**Doug Moore:** Fluorescent sodalite; Doug Moore is known throughout the world for his knowledge of and passion for geology and for gem and mineral prospecting and collecting. Doug is always doing something to help promote and educate about the rockhounding hobby. Doug showcases his outstanding photographic talents in the Fluorescent Sodalite chapter.

# Addditional Subject Matter Experts

Each of these people contributed in a material way to my knowledge and understanding of hobby gem and mineral prospecting. Many thanks to all of you!

Bob Kalis: Petoskey stones and other Michigan fossils

Greg Tamillo: Minnesota and Wisconsin gold prospecting

Jim Ericson: Keokuk geodes

Ken Flood (Keweenaw Gem & Gift): copper and Petoskey stone lapidary

Steve Melbrech: Teepee Canyon agates

Dave Reed: Fairburn agates

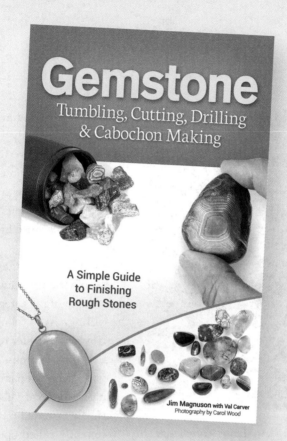

# SIMPLE INSTRUCTIONS, PROFESSIONAL RESULTS!

Gemstones are naturally beautiful, but you can make them glisten and shine. This beginner's guide covers all the techniques you need to know: tumbling, cutting, face polishing and more. By following the authors' simple approach, you'll create finished stones worthy of displaying, selling or making into jewelry.

## Book Features

- pertains to a wide range of popular gemstones, from agates to turquoise
- prevents frustration, with detailed photos and easy-to-follow instructions
- offers helful tips from the authors' years of experience
- provides information about recommended equipment and supplies
- briefly introduces jewelry making, with seven simple jewelry projects

# ABOUT THE AUTHOR

For author Jim Magnuson, rock-hounding is not only a hobby, but it's also a serious and rewarding avocation that helps him connect with nature. He has been an avid hunter and student of various gems, minerals, and fossils since his childhood, when he first began to hunt for stones in his native state of Illinois. These experiences taught Jim the importance of persistence and the willingness to follow the road less traveled in order to find unique or rare kinds of rocks. Jim also enjoys sharing his passion through writing, both creatively and from a practically oriented process perspective. Because of Jim's in-depth knowledge, he is frequently called upon to present to groups such as rock and mineral clubs, geological societies, and educational institutions that focus on outdoor and environmental interests. In addition to Jim's passion for prospecting and hunting, he also likes to perform various lapidary arts with the stones that he finds, and he has a small business making and selling custom-polished stones and jewelry pieces. Finally, Jim enjoys creating photographic illustrations that are up close and personal for prospecting, hunting, and lapidary work. Jim was a photographer for his high school and college newspapers and yearbooks, where he focused on student activities that created perspectives on campus life. This experience has helped Jim capture unique and compelling photographic images for modern-day gem and mineral prospecting.